OTHELLO

William Shakespeare

Prestwick House

LITERARY TOUCHSTONE CLASSICS™

P.O. Box 658 Clayton, Delaware 19938 • www.prestwickhouse.com

SENIOR EDITOR: Paul Moliken

EDITOR: Darlene Gilmore

DESIGN/PHOTOGRAPHY: Wendy Smith

PRODUCTION: Larry Knox

Prestwick House
LITERARY TOUCHSTONE CLASSICS™

P.O. BOX 658 • CLAYTON, DELAWARE 19938
TEL: 1.800.932.4593
FAX: 1.888.718.9333
WEB: www.prestwickhouse.com

Prestwick House Teaching Units,™ Activity Packs,™ and Response Journals™ are the perfect complement for these editions. To purchase teaching resources for this book, visit www.prestwickhouse.com.

ISBN   978-1-58049-590-5

CONTENTS

Strategies for Understanding Shakespeare's Language

1. **When reading verse, note the appropriate phrasing and intonation.**

    DO NOT PAUSE AT THE END OF A LINE unless there is a mark of punctuation. Shakespearean verse has a rhythm of its own, and once a reader gets used to it, the rhythm becomes very natural to speak in and read. Beginning readers often find it helpful to read a short pause at a comma and a long pause for a period, colon, semicolon, dash, or question mark.

    Here's an example from *The Merchant of Venice,* Act IV, Scene i:

    > The quality of mercy is not strain'd, (*short pause*)
    > It droppeth as the gentle rain from heaven
    > Upon the place beneath: (*long pause*) it is twice blest; (*long pause*)
    > It blesseth him that gives, (*short pause*) and him that takes; (*long pause*)
    > 'Tis mightiest in the mighties; (*long pause*) it becomes
    > The throned monarch better than his crown; (*long pause*)

2. **Read from punctuation mark to punctuation mark for meaning.**

    In addition to helping you read aloud, punctuation marks define units of thought. Try to understand each unit as you read, keeping in mind that periods, colons, semicolons, and question marks signal the end of a thought. Here's an example from *The Taming of the Shrew,* Act I, Scene i:

    > Luc. Tranio, I saw her coral lips to move,
    >   And with her breath she did perfume the air;
    >   Sacred, and sweet, was all I saw in her.
    > Tra. Nay, then, 'tis time to stir him from his
    >   trance.
    >   I pray, awake, sir: if you love the maid,
    >   Bend thoughts and wits to achieve her.

The first unit of thought is from "Tranio" to "air":
He saw her lips move, and her breath perfumed the air.

The second thought ("Sacred, and sweet...") re-emphasizes the first.

Tranio replies that Lucentio needs to awaken from his trance and try to win "the maid." These two sentences can be considered one unit of thought.

3. In an **inverted sentence**, the verb comes before the subject. Some lines will be easier to understand if you put the subject first and reword the sentence. For example, look at the line below:

   "Never was seen so black a day as this:" (*Romeo and Juliet*, Act IV, Scene v)

   You can change its inverted pattern so it is more easily understood:

   "A day as black as this was never seen:"

4. An **ellipsis** occurs when a word or phrase is left out. In *Romeo and Juliet*, Benvolio asks Romeo's father and mother if they know the problem that is bothering their son. Romeo's father answers:

   "I neither know it nor can learn of him" (*Romeo and Juliet*, Act I, Scene i)

   This sentence can easily be understood to mean,

   "I neither know [the cause of] it,
   nor can [I] learn [about it from] him."

5. As you read longer speeches, keep track of the subject, verb, and object—*who* did *what* to *whom*.

   In the clauses below, note the subject, verbs, and objects:

   Ross: The king hath happily received, Macbeth,
       The news of thy success: and when he reads
       Thy personal venture in the rebel's fight... (*Macbeth*, Act I, Scene iii)

   1st clause: *The king hath happily received, Macbeth,/The news of thy success:*
   SUBJECT – The king
   VERB – has received
   OBJECT – the news [of Macbeth's success]

2nd clause: *and when he reads/thy personal venture in the rebel's fight,*
SUBJECT – he [the king]
VERB – reads
OBJECT – [about] your venture

In addition to following the subject, verb, and object of a clause, you also need to track pronoun references. In the following soliloquy, Romeo, who is madly in love with Juliet, secretly observes her as she steps out on her balcony. To help you keep track of the pronoun references, we've made margin notes. (Note that the feminine pronoun sometimes refers to Juliet, but sometimes does not.)

> But, soft! what light through yonder window breaks?
> It is the east, and Juliet is the sun!
> Arise, fair sun, and kill the envious moon,
> Who* is already sick and pale with grief,   *"Who" refers to the moon.*
> That thou her* maid* art more fair than she:*   *"thou her maid" refers*
> *to Juliet, the sun.*
> *"she" and "her" refer to the moon.*

In tracking the line of action in a passage, it is useful to identify the main thoughts that are being expressed and paraphrase them. Note the following passage in which Hamlet expresses his feelings about the death of his father and the remarriage of his mother:

> O God! a beast that wants discourse of reason
> Would have mourn'd longer—married with my uncle,
> My father's brother, but no more like my father
> Than I to Hercules. (*Hamlet*, Act I, Scene ii)

Paraphrasing the three main points, we find that Hamlet is saying:

- a mindless beast would have mourned the death of its mate longer than my mother did
- she married my uncle, my father's brother
- my uncle is not at all like my father

If you are having trouble understanding Shakespeare, the first rule is to read it out loud, just as an actor rehearsing would have to do. That will help you understand how one thought is connected to another.

6. Shakespeare frequently uses **metaphor** to illustrate an idea in a unique way. Pay careful attention to the two dissimilar objects or ideas being compared.

In *Macbeth*, Duncan, the king says:

> I have begun to plant thee, and will labour
> To make thee full of growing. (*Macbeth*, Act I, Scene v)

The king compares Macbeth to a tree he can plant and watch grow.

7. An **allusion** is a reference to some event, person, place, or artistic work, not directly explained or discussed by the writer; it relies on the reader's familiarity with the item referred to. Allusion is a quick way of conveying information or presenting an image. In the following lines, Romeo alludes to Diana, goddess of the hunt and of chastity, and to Cupid's arrow (love).

> ROMEO: Well, in that hit you miss: she'll not be hit
> with Cupid's arrow, she hath Dian's wit;
> and in strong proof of chastity well arm'd
> (*Romeo and Juliet*, Act I, Scene i)

8. Contracted words are words in which a letter has been left out. Some that frequently appear:

be't	on't	wi'
do't	t'	'sblood
'gainst	ta'en	i'
'tis	e'en	
'bout	know'st	'twill
	ne'er	o' o'er

9. Archaic, obsolete, and familiar words with unfamiliar definitions may also cause problems.

- **Archaic Words:** Some archaic words, like *thee, thou, thy,* and *thine,* are instantly understandable, while others, like *betwixt,* cause a momentary pause.

- **Obsolete Words:** If it were not for the notes in a Shakespeare text, obsolete words could be a problem; words like *beteem* are usually not found in student dictionaries. In these situations, however, a quick glance at the book's notes will solve the problem.

- **Familiar Words with Unfamiliar Definitions:** Another problem is those familiar words whose definitions have changed. Because readers think they know the word, they do not check the notes. For example, in this comment from *Much Ado About Nothing*, Act I, Scene i, the word *an* means "if":

BEATRICE: Scratching could not make it worse, *an* 'twere such
a face as yours were.

For this kind of word, we have included margin notes.

10. **Wordplay—puns, double entendres**, and **malapropisms**:

- A **pun** is a literary device that achieves humor or emphasis by playing on ambiguities. Two distinct meanings are suggested either by the same word or by two similar-sounding words.

- A **double entendre** is a kind of pun in which a word or phrase has a second, usually sexual, meaning.

- A **malapropism** occurs when a character mistakenly uses a word that he or she has confused with another word. In *Romeo and Juliet*, the Nurse tells Romeo that she needs to have a "confidence" with him, when she should have said "conference." Mockingly, Benvolio then says she probably will "indite" (rather than "invite") Romeo to dinner.

11. **Shakespeare's Language**:

Our final word on Shakespeare's language is adapted by special permission from Ralph Alan Cohen's book *Shakesfear and How to Cure It—A Guide to Teaching Shakespeare*.

What's so hard about Shakespeare's language? Many students come to Shakespeare's language assuming that the language of his period is substantially different from ours. In fact, 98% of the words in Shakespeare are current-usage English words. So why does it sometimes seem hard to read Shakespeare? There are three main reasons:

- Originally, Shakespeare wrote the words for an actor to illustrate them as he spoke. In short, the play you have at hand was meant for the stage, not for the page.

- Shakespeare had the same love of reforming and rearranging words in such places as hip-hop and sportscasting today. His plays reflect an excitement about language and an inventiveness that becomes enjoyable once the reader gets into the spirit of it.

- Since Shakespeare puts all types of people on stage, those characters will include some who are pompous, some who are devious, some who are boring, and some who are crazy, and all of these will speak in ways that are sometimes trying. Modern playwrights creating similar characters have them speak in similarly challenging ways.

12. **Stage Directions:**

Shakespeare's stagecraft went hand-in-hand with his wordcraft. For that reason, we believe it is important for the reader to know which stage directions are modern and which derive from Shakespeare's earliest text—the single-play Quartos or the Folio, the first collected works (1623). All stage directions appear in italics, but the brackets enclose modern additions to the stage directions. Readers may assume that the unbracketed stage directions appear in the Quarto and/or Folio versions of the play.

13. **Scene Locations:**

Shakespeare imagined his plays, first and foremost, on the stage of his outdoor or indoor theatre. The original printed versions of the plays do not give imaginary scene locations, except when they are occasionally mentioned in the dialogue. As an aid to the reader, this edition *does* include scene locations at the beginning of each scene, but puts all such locations in brackets to remind the reader that *this is not what Shakespeare envisioned and only possibly what he imagined.*

Reading Pointers for Sharper Insights

As you read, look for the themes and elements described below:

Contrasts:
Animals, animal instincts vs. the divine or "higher" nature:
- Iago plays on other characters' emotions by suggesting that Othello is more animal than human. Pay special attention to any mention of animals, beasts, and hunting.
- Desdemona is often called "divine" by Othello and others. Note the contrast between high and low, and between heaven and hell, both within the play and within individual characters. What makes a person's "baser" nature come out? Where does Iago's nature fit in this scheme?
- Racial elements also provide a point of contrast and conflict that the characters are quick to use to exploit when it is convenient for them to use it to denigrate Othello.

Soldiers and civilians:
- Othello admits that he knows little of the "civilized" world; his place is in battle. He considers himself unrefined. Who else brings up the different worlds of war and peace, rude and polite? Do these worlds ever intersect?

Self-knowledge:
Until he begins to suspect Desdemona, Othello is able to remain calm in the midst of chaotic situations (when he is dragged before Brabantio, for instance, or when he comes upon the brawl in Cyprus).

Once he has been infected by doubt, however, he cannot go back to his previous beliefs, no matter how much he would like to. His rage skews his judgment and colors everything he sees—notice how the handkerchief, a cherished token of his courtship and marriage, takes on new symbolism when his faith begins to unravel. How clearly does Othello see his own fall?

Dramatic irony:

Iago makes his plans known to the audience through asides—addresses to the audience that the other characters cannot hear, or when alone on stage. The tension between the ignorance of Othello, Desdemona, Cassio, and Roderigo and our knowledge of what is going to happen to them heightens the drama of the play.

Double entendre:

A double entendre is a play on words, especially one having sexual overtones. Iago uses many of these, especially when he wishes to poison the mind of Othello with doubts.

Language:

Follow Othello's language as he falls apart, remembering that, in Shakespeare's time, "You" was used for polite address, while "Thee" and "thou" indicated a lack of formality.

OTHELLO

WILLIAM SHAKESPEARE

DRAMATIS PERSONAE

DUKE OF VENICE.
BRABANTIO, [A senator], father to Desdemona
GRATIANO [brother to Brabantio].
LODOVICO [kinsman to Brabantio]. } Two noble Venetians
OTHELLO, the Moor [in the military service of Venice].
CASSIO, an honourable lieutenant [to Othello].
IAGO, [an ensign to Othello], a villian.
RODERIGO, a Venetian gentleman.
MONTANO, governor of Cyprus [before Othello].

Clown [servant to Othello].
DESDEMONA, wife to Othello.
EMILIA, wife to Iago.
BIANCA, a courtezan [mistress to Cassio].

[Other] SENATORS, SAILORS, GENTLEMEN OF CYPRUS
[OFFICERS, MESSENGERS, MUSICIANS].

*[The first act takes place in Venice. The rest of the play takes place
in a seaport in Cyprus.]*

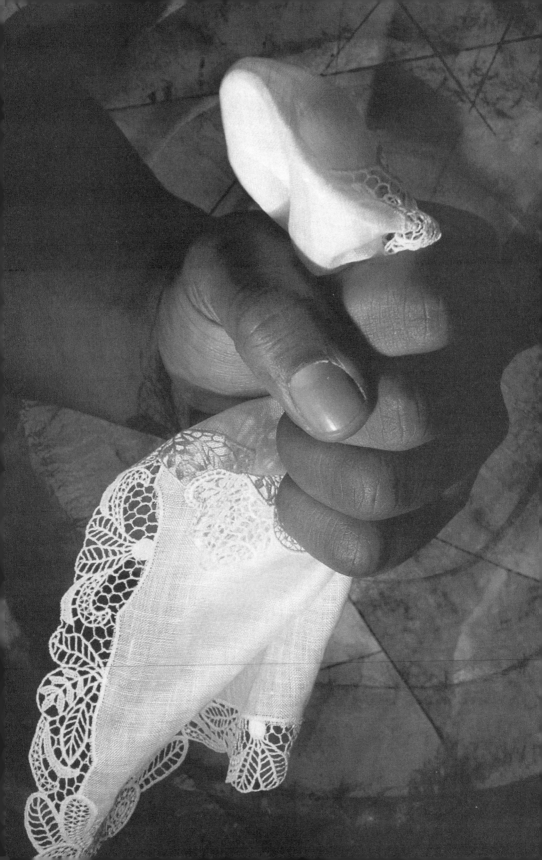

ACT I

SCENE I
[Venice. A Street.]

Enter Roderigo and Iago.

Rod: Tush, never tell me! I take it much unkindly
    That thou, Iago, who hast had my purse
    As if the strings were thine, shouldst know of this.
Iago: 'Sblood, but you will not hear me.
5   If ever I did dream of such a matter,
    Abhor me.
Rod: Thou told'st me thou didst hold him in thy hate.
Iago: Despise me, if I do not. Three great ones of the city,
    In personal suit to make me his lieutenant,
10   Offcapp'd[1] to him; and, by the faith of man,
    I know my price, I am worth no worse a place.
    But he, as loving his own pride and purposes,
    Evades them with a bombast[2] circumstance[3]
    Horribly stuff'd with epithets of war,
15   And, in conclusion,
    Nonsuits[4] my mediators;[5] for, "Certes," says he,
    "I have already chose my officer."
    And what was he?
    Forsooth, a great arithmetician,
20   One Michael Cassio, a Florentine
    A fellow almost damn'd in a fair wife[6]
    That never set a squadron in the field,
    Nor the division of a battle knows
    More than a spinster; unless[7] the bookish theoric,[8]
25   Wherein[9] the toga'd consuls[10] can propose
    As masterly[11] as he; mere prattle[12] without practice,
    Is all his soldiership. But he, sir, had the election;[13]

[1] *tipped their hats*

[2] *overdone*

[3] *roundabout speech*

[4] *denies*

[5] *people appealing on my behalf*

[6] *[Cassio is unmarried, so the meaning of this line is mysterious.]*

[7] *except*

[8] *abstract theory, [as opposed to reality]*

[9] *about which*

[10] *bureaucrats*

[11] *knowledgeably*

[12] *chatter*

[13] *choice*

15

[14]military ability

[15][Iago compares himself to a ship on a calm sea.]

[16]one who makes petty calculations

[17]coin-counter

[18]low-ranking officer

[19]personal favor

[20]i.e., process of promotion

[21]was automatically promoted

[22]bound

[23]kneeling

[24]loving

[25]feed

[26]dismissed

[27]appearances

[28]favor

[29]personal

[30]form

    And I,—of whom his eyes had seen the proof[14]
    At Rhodes, at Cyprus, and on other grounds
30   Christian and heathen,—must be belee'd and calm'd[15]
    By debitor and creditor.[16] This countercaster,[17]
    He, in good time, must his lieutenant be,
    And I—God bless the mark!—his Moorship's ancient.[18]
    ROD: By heaven, I rather would have been his hangman.
35 IAGO: Why, there's no remedy. 'Tis the curse of service,
    Preferment goes by letter and affection,[19]
    And not by old gradation,[20] where each second
    Stood heir to the first.[21] Now, sir, be judge yourself
    Whether I in any just term am affined[22]
40   To love the Moor.
    ROD: I would not follow him then.
    IAGO: O, sir, content you.
    I follow him to serve my turn upon him:
    We cannot all be masters, nor all masters
45   Cannot be truly follow'd. You shall mark
    Many a duteous and kneecrooking[23] knave,
    That doting on[24] his own obsequious bondage
    Wears out his time, much like his master's ass,
    For naught but provender;[25] and, when he's old, cashier'd.[26]
50   Whip me such honest knaves. Others there are,
    Who, trimm'd in forms and visages[27] of duty,
    Keep yet their hearts attending on themselves,
    And throwing but shows of service on their lords
    Do well thrive by them; and when they have lined their
55   coats
    Do themselves homage.[28] These fellows have some soul,
    And such a one do I profess myself.
    For, sir,
    It is as sure as you are Roderigo,
60   Were I the Moor, I would not be Iago.
    In following him, I follow but myself;
    Heaven is my judge, not I for love and duty,
    But seeming so, for my peculiar[29] end.
    For when my outward action doth demonstrate
65   The native act and figure of my heart
    In complement[30] extern, 'tis not long after
    But I will wear my heart upon my sleeve

For daws[31] to peck at: I am not what I am.

Rod: *[Aside]* What a full fortune does the thicklips owe,[32]

70   If he can carry't[33] thus!

Iago: Call up her father,   *Upset father*

        Rouse him:—make after him, poison his delight,   *Pester him,*

        Proclaim him in the streets, incense her kinsmen,   *spread*

        And, though he in a fertile climate dwell,[34]   *rumors*

75   Plague him with flies. Though that his joy be joy,   *irritate him*

        Yet throw such changes of vexation on't

        As it may lose some color.   *happiness with pride*

Rod: Here is her father's house; I'll call aloud.

Iago: Do; with like timorous[35] accent and dire yell

80   As when, by night and negligence, the fire

        Is spied in populous cities.

Rod: What, ho, Brabantio! Signior Brabantio, ho!

Iago: Awake! What, ho, Brabantio! thieves! thieves! thieves!

        Look to your house, your daughter, and your bags!

85   Thieves! thieves!

Brabantio appears above, at a window.

Brab: What is the reason of this terrible summons?

        What is the matter there?

Rod: Signior, is all your family within?

Iago: Are your doors lock'd?

90 Brab: Why? Wherefore ask you this?

Iago: 'Zounds, sir, you're robb'd! For shame, put on your

        gown;   *About to break*

        Your heart is burst, you have lost half your soul;

        Even now, now, very now, an old black ram

95   Is tupping[36] your white ewe. Arise, arise!   *Racist*

        Awake the snorting[37] citizens with the bell,

        Or else the devil will make a grandsire of you.

        Arise, I say!

Brab: What, have you lost your wits?

100 Rod: Most reverend signior, do you know my voice?

Brab: Not I. What are you?

Rod: My name is Roderigo.

Brab: The worser welcome.

        I have charged thee not to haunt about my doors: *Get out*

---

[31]*crows*

[32]*own*

[33]*pull it off*

[34]*i.e., though he is fortunate*

[35]*frightened*

[36]*mating with*

[37]*snoring*

105   In honest plainness thou hast heard me say
       My daughter is not for thee; and now, in madness,—

[38]mind altering   Being full of supper and distempering[38] draughts,—
       Upon malicious bravery, dost thou come
       To start my quiet.

110   ROD: Sir, sir, sir—
       BRAB: But thou must needs be sure
       My spirit and my place have in them power
       To make this bitter to thee.
       ROD: Patience, good sir.

115   BRAB: What tell'st thou me of robbing? This is Venice;

[39]farm   My house is not a grange.[39]
       ROD: Most grave Brabantio,
       In simple and pure soul I come to you.
       IAGO: 'Zounds, sir, you are one of those that will not serve

120   God, if the devil bid you. Because we come to do you
       service and you think we are ruffians, you'll have your

[40]African   daughter covered with a Barbary[40] horse; you'll have your
[41]stallions   nephews neigh to you; you'll have coursers[41] for cousins,
[42]small horses   and gennets[42] for germans.

125   BRAB: What profane wretch art thou?
       IAGO: I am one, sir, that comes to tell you your daughter and
       the Moor are now making the beast with two backs.
       BRAB: Thou art a villain.
       IAGO: You are—a senator.

130   BRAB: This thou shalt answer; I know thee, Roderigo.
       ROD: Sir, I will answer any thing. But, I beseech you,
       If't be your pleasure and most wise consent,
       As partly I find it is, that your fair daughter,

[43]middle   At this odd-even[43] and dull watch o' the night,

135   Transported, with no worse nor better guard

[44]boatman   But with a knave of common hire, a gondolier,[44]
       To the gross clasps of a lascivious Moor—
       If this be known to you, and your allowance,
       We then have done you bold and saucy wrongs;

140   But, if you know not this, my manners tell me

[45]unfair criticism   We have your wrong rebuke.[45] Do not believe

[46]against   That, from[46] the sense of all civility,
       I thus would play and trifle with your reverence.
       Your daughter, if you have not given her leave,

145 I say again, hath made a gross revolt,
  Tying her duty, beauty, wit, and fortunes
  In an extravagant and wheeling stranger
  Of here and everywhere. Straight satisfy yourself:
  If she be in her chamber or your house,
150 Let loose on me the justice of the state
  For thus deluding you.
 Brab: Strike on the tinder, ho!
  Give me a taper! Call up all my people!
  This accident is not unlike my dream;
155 Belief of it oppresses me already.
  Light, I say, light!   [Exit.]
 Iago: Farewell, for I must leave you.
  It seems not meet,[47] nor wholesome[48] to my place,
  To be produced—as, if I stay, I shall—
160 Against the Moor. For I do know, the state,
  However this[49] may gall him with some check,[50]
  Cannot with safety cast[51] him; for he's embark'd
  With such loud[52] reason to the Cyprus' wars,
  Which even now stands in act,[53] that, for their souls,
165 Another of his fathom[54] they have none
  To lead their business; in which regard,
  Though I do hate him as I do hell-pains,
  Yet for necessity of present life,
  I must show out a flag and sign of love,
170 Which is indeed but sign. That you shall surely find him,
  Lead to the Sagittary[55] the raised search,
  And there will I be with him. So farewell. Exit.

Enter Brabantio in his nightgown, and Servants with torches.

 Brab: It is too true an evil: gone she is,
  And what's to come of my despised time
175 Is nought but bitterness.—Now, Roderigo,
  Where didst thou see her? —O unhappy girl!—
  With the Moor, say'st thou?—Who would be a father!
  How didst thou know 'twas she? —O, she deceives me
  Past thought!—What said she to you?—Get more tapers.
180 Raise all my kindred. —Are they married, think you?
 Rod: Truly, I think they are.

[47]*fitting*

[48]*beneficial*

[49]*the public
questioning by
Brabantio*

[50]*demerit*

[51]*get rid of*

[52]*urgent*

[53]*the process*

[54]*capacity*

[55]*the name of a
lodging-house*

BRAB: O heaven!—How got she out? —O treason of the
    blood!
Fathers, from hence trust not your daughters' minds

⁵⁶spells

185 By what you see them act. Are there not charms⁵⁶
By which the property of youth and maidhood
May be abused? Have you not read, Roderigo,
Of some such thing?
ROD: Yes, sir, I have indeed.   *married*

190 BRAB: Call up my brother. —O, would you had had her!—
Some one way, some another.—Do you know

⁵⁷find

Where we may apprehend her and the Moor?
ROD: I think I can discover⁵⁷ him, if you please
To get good guard, and go along with me.

195 BRAB: Pray you, lead on. At every house I'll call;
I may command at most.—Get weapons, ho!

⁵⁸efforts

And raise some special officers of night.—
On, good Roderigo,—I'll deserve your pains.⁵⁸

Exeunt.

SCENE II
[Another street.]

Enter Othello, Iago, and Attendants with torches.

IAGO: Though in the trade of war I have slain men,

⁵⁹deliberate

Yet do I hold it very stuff o' the conscience
To do no contrived⁵⁹ murder. I lack iniquity⁶⁰

⁶⁰wickedness

Sometimes to do me service. Nine or ten times

⁶¹stabbed

5 I had thought to have yerk'd⁶¹ him here under the ribs.
OTHELLO: 'Tis better as it is.

⁶²chattered on

IAGO: Nay, but he prated⁶²
And spoke such scurvy⁶³ and provoking terms

⁶³unpleasant

Against your honor

⁶⁴tolerate

10 That, with the little godliness I have,
I did full hard forbear⁶⁴ him. But I pray you, sir,

⁶⁵securely

Are you fast⁶⁵ married? Be assured of this, *Be Forever!*
That the magnifico is much beloved,

⁶⁶possibly

And hath in his effect a voice potential⁶⁶

15 As double as the Duke's. He will divorce you,
Or put upon you what restraint and grievance

The law, with all his might to enforce it on,
Will give him cable.[67]

OTHELLO: Let him do his spite.

20   My services, which I have done the signiory,[68]
Shall out-tongue his complaints. 'Tis yet to know—
Which, when I know that boasting is an honor,
I shall promulgate[69]—I fetch my life and being
From men of royal siege;[70] and my demerits[71]

25   May speak unbonneted[72] to as proud a fortune
As this that I have reach'd. For know, Iago,
But[73] that I love the gentle Desdemona,
I would not my unhoused[74] free condition *Wou[ld] [no]t lose freedom?*
Put into circumscription[75] and confine

30   For the sea's worth. But, look! What lights come yond?

IAGO: Those are the raised[76] father and his friends.
You were best go in.

OTHELLO: Not I; I must be found.
My parts, my title, and my perfect soul

35   Shall manifest[77] me rightly. Is it they?

IAGO: By Janus, I think no.
Two faces

Enter Cassio and certain Officers with torches.

OTHELLO: The servants of the Duke?
And my lieutenant?
The goodness of the night upon you, friends!

40   What is the news?

CASSIO: The Duke does greet you, general,
And he requires your haste-post-haste appearance,
Even on the instant. *hurry*

OTHELLO: What is the matter, think you?

45 CASSIO: Something from Cyprus, as I may divine;[78]
It is a business of some heat. The galleys
Have sent a dozen sequent[79] messengers
This very night at one another's heels; *ships*
And many of the consuls, raised and met,

50   Are at the Duke's already. You have been hotly call'd for;
When, being not at your lodging to be found,
The Senate hath sent about three quests
To search you out. *Trying to find you*

OTHELLO: 'Tis well I am found by you.

[67]ability	
[68]government of Venice	
[69]make known	
[70]seat	
[71]merits	
[72]plainly	
[73]except	
[74]unconfined	
[75]limit	
[76]awakened	
[77]show	
[78]guess	
[79]consecutive	

55   I will but spend a word here in the house
         And go with you.   [Exit.]
      CASSIO: Ancient, what makes he here?
      IAGO: Faith, he tonight hath boarded a land carack;[80]
         If it prove lawful prize, he's made forever.
60   CASSIO: I do not understand.
      IAGO: He's married.
      CASSIO: To who?

      [Reenter Othello.]

      IAGO: Marry, to—Come, captain, will you go?
      OTHELLO: Have with you.
65   CASSIO: Here comes another troop to seek for you.
      IAGO: It is Brabantio.—General, be advised;
         He comes to bad intent.

      Enter Brabantio, Roderigo, and Officers with torches
         and weapons.

      OTHELLO: Holla! Stand there!
      ROD: Signior, it is the Moor.
70   BRAB: Down with him, thief!   They draw on both sides.
      IAGO: You, Roderigo! Come, sir, I am for you.
      OTHELLO: Keep up your bright swords, for the dew will rust
            them.—
         Good signior, you shall more command with years
75   Than with your weapons.
      BRAB: O thou foul thief, where hast thou stow'd my
            daughter?
         Damn'd as thou art, thou hast enchanted her,
         For I'll refer me to all things of sense,
80   If she in chains of magic were not bound,
         Whether a maid so tender, fair, and happy,
         So opposite to marriage that she shunn'd
         The wealthy, curled darlings of our nation,
         Would ever have, to incur a general mock,
85   Run from her guardage to the sooty bosom
         Of such a thing as thou—to fear, not to delight.
         Judge me the world, if 'tis not gross[81] in sense
         That thou hast practiced on her with foul charms;

[80]*ship*

[81]*abundantly clear*

Abused her delicate youth with drugs or minerals
90 That weaken motion:[82]—I'll have't disputed on;
'Tis probable, and palpable[83] to thinking.
I therefore apprehend and do attach[84] thee
For an abuser of the world, a practicer
Of arts inhibited and out of warrant.[85]—
95 Lay hold upon him. If he do resist,
Subdue him at his peril.
OTHELLO: Hold your hands,
Both you of my inclining,[86] and the rest:
Were it my cue to fight, I should have known it
100 Without a prompter.—Where will you that I go
To answer this your charge?
BRAB: To prison; till fit time
Of law and course of direct session,
Call thee to answer.
105 OTHELLO: What if I do obey?
How may the Duke be therewith satisfied,
Whose messengers are here about my side,
Upon some present business of the state
To bring me to him?
110 FIRST OFFICER: 'Tis true, most worthy signior;
The Duke's in council, and your noble self,
I am sure, is sent for.
BRAB: How? The Duke in council?
In this time of the night?—Bring him away;
115 Mine's not an idle cause. The Duke himself,
Or any of my brothers of the state,
Cannot but feel this wrong as 'twere their own;
For if such actions may have passage free,[87]
Bond-slaves and pagans shall our statesmen be.

Exeunt.

[82]*willpower*

[83]*very likely*

[84]*arrest*

[85]*law*

[86]*way of thinking*

[87]*i.e., be allowed*

SCENE III
[A council chamber.]

*Enter Duke and Senators, set at a table with lights
and attendants.*

[88]*consistency*

DUKE: There is no composition[88] in these news
 That gives them credit.
FIRST SENATOR: Indeed they are disproportion'd;
 My letters say a hundred and seven galleys.
5 DUKE: And mine, a hundred and forty.
SECOND SENATOR: And mine, two hundred.
 But though they jump[89] not on a just[90] account—
 As in these cases, where the aim reports,
 'Tis oft with difference—yet do they all confirm
10 A Turkish fleet, and bearing up to Cyprus.
DUKE: Nay, it is possible enough to judgement:
 I do not so secure[91] me in the error,
 But the main article I do approve
 In fearful sense.
15 SAILOR: *[Within.]* What, ho! What, ho! What, ho!

           [Enter Sailor.]

FIRST OFFICER: A messenger from the galleys.
DUKE: Now, what's the business?
SAILOR: The Turkish preparation[92] makes for Rhodes;
 So was I bid report here to the state
20 By Signior Angelo.
DUKE: How say you by this change?
FIRST SENATOR: This cannot be,
 By no assay[93] of reason; 'tis a pageant[94]
 To keep us in false gaze. When we consider
25 The importancy of Cyprus to the Turk;
 And let ourselves again but understand
 That as it more concerns the Turk than Rhodes,
 So may he with more facile question bear it,[95]
 For that it stands not in such warlike brace,
30 But altogether lacks the abilities[96]
 That Rhodes is dress'd in;—
 If we make thought of this,
 We must not think the Turk is so unskillful

[89]*agree*

[90]*correct*

[91]*comfort*

[92]*force*

[93]*test*

[94]*show*

[95]*so long as he
(the Turk) may
take Cyprus more
easily*

[96]*defenses*

To leave that latest which concerns him first,
35   Neglecting an attempt of ease and gain,
To wake and wage a danger profitless.
DUKE: Nay, in all confidence, he's not for Rhodes.
FIRST OFFICER: Here is more news.

[Enter a Messenger.]

MESSENGER: The Ottomites, reverend and gracious,
40   Steering with due course toward the isle of Rhodes,
Have there injointed[97] them with an after fleet.   [97]*joined*
FIRST SENATOR: Ay, so I thought. How many, as you guess?
MESSENGER: Of thirty sail; and now they do restem[98]   [98]*retrace*
Their backward course, bearing with frank appearance
45   Their purposes toward Cyprus. Signior Montano,
Your trusty and most valiant servitor,
With his free duty recommends you thus,
And prays you to believe him.
DUKE: 'Tis certain then for Cyprus.
50   Marcus Luccicos, is not he in town?
FIRST SENATOR: He's now in Florence.
DUKE: Write from us to him, post-post-haste dispatch.
FIRST SENATOR: Here comes Brabantio and the valiant Moor.

Enter Brabantio, Othello, Iago, Roderigo, and Officers.

DUKE: Valiant Othello, we must straight employ you
55   Against the general enemy Ottoman.
I did not see you; welcome, gentle signior;
We lack'd your counsel and your help tonight.
BRAB: So did I yours. Good your Grace, pardon me:
Neither my place nor aught I heard of business
60   Hath raised me from my bed, nor doth the general care
Take hold on me; for my particular grief
Is of so floodgate[99] and o'erbearing nature   [99]*overwhelming*
That it engluts[100] and swallows other sorrows,   [100]*stuffs itself on*
And it is still itself.
65 DUKE: Why, what's the matter?
BRAB: My daughter! O, my daughter!
ALL: Dead?

[101]*cheating sales-men*

[102]*her nature*

[103]*without*

[104]*cheated*

[105]*judgment*

[106]*unpolished*

[107]*plain*

BRAB: Ay, to me. _dead_

She is abused, stol'n from me and corrupted

70   By spells and medicines bought of mountebanks;[101]

For nature[102] so preposterously to err,

Being not deficient, blind, or lame of sense,

Sans[103] witchcraft could not.

DUKE: Whoe'er he be that in this foul proceeding

75   Hath thus beguiled[104] your daughter of herself

And you of her, the bloody book of law

You shall yourself read in the bitter letter   *Pay for it + decide*

After your own sense.[105]

BRAB: Humbly I thank your Grace.

80   Here is the man, this Moor; whom now, it seems,

Your special mandate for the state affairs

Hath hither brought.

ALL: We are very sorry for't.

DUKE: What in your own part can you say to this?

85   BRAB: Nothing, but this is so.

OTHELLO: Most potent, grave, and reverend signiors,

My very noble and approved good masters,

That I have ta'en away this old man's daughter,

It is most true; true, I have married her;   *Anadiplosis*

90   The very head and front of my offending

Hath this extent, no more. Rude[106] am I in my speech,

And little blest with the soft phrase of peace;

For since these arms of mine had seven years' pith,

Till now some nine moons wasted, they have used

95   Their dearest action in the tented field,

And little of this great world can I speak,

More than pertains to feats of broil and battle;

And therefore little shall I grace my cause

In speaking for myself. Yet, by your gracious patience,

100   I will a round unvarnish'd[107] tale deliver

Of my whole course of love: what drugs, what charms,

What conjuration, and what mighty magic —

For such proceeding I am charged withal   *Anaphora*

I won his daughter.

105   BRAB: A maiden never bold; *Good*

Of spirit so still and quiet that her motion *blush at something*

Blush'd at herself; and she—in spite of nature,

　　　Of years, of country, credit, everything—
　　　To fall in love with what she fear'd to look on! *[handwritten note]*
110　　It is judgement maim'd and most imperfect,
　　　That will confess perfection so could err
　　　Against all rules of nature, I therefore vouch again,
　　　That with some mixtures powerful o'er the blood,
　　　Or with some dram[108] conjured to this effect,
115　　He wrought upon her.

　　DUKE: To vouch this, is no proof, *[handwritten note]*
　　　Without more certain and more overt test
　　　Than these thin habits and poor likelihoods
　　　Of modern[109] seeming do prefer against him.
120　FIRST SENATOR: But, Othello, speak.
　　　Did you by indirect and forced courses
　　　Subdue and poison this young maid's affections?
　　　Or came it by request, and such fair question
　　　As soul to soul affordeth?
125　OTHELLO: I do beseech you,
　　　Send for the lady to the Sagittary,
　　　And let her speak of me before her father:
　　　If you do find me foul in her report,
　　　The trust, the office I do hold of you,
130　　Not only take away, but let your sentence
　　　Even fall upon my life.

　　DUKE: Fetch Desdemona hither.　　　　　*Exit two or three.*

　　OTHELLO: Ancient, conduct them; you best know the place.

　　　　　　　　　　　　　　　　　　[Exit Iago.]

　　　And till she come, as truly as to heaven
135　　I do confess the vices of my blood,
　　　So justly to your grave ears I'll present
　　　How I did thrive in this fair lady's love
　　　And she in mine.

　　DUKE: Say it, Othello.

140　OTHELLO: Her father loved me, oft invited me,
　　　Still question'd me the story of my life
　　　From year to year, the battles, sieges, fortunes,
　　　That I have pass'd.
　　　I ran it through, even from my boyish days
145　　To the very moment that he bade me tell it:
　　　Wherein I spake of most disastrous chances,

[108]*liquid potion*

[109]*ordinary*

[110]*desperate*

[111]*escapes*

[112]*release*

[113]*behavior*

[114]*caves*

[115]*finish*

[116]*favorable*

[117]*expand upon*

[118]*bits and pieces*

[119]*attentively*

[120]*cheat*

Of moving accidents by flood and field,
Of hairbreadth[110] 'scapes[111] i' the imminent deadly breach,
Of being taken by the insolent foe,

150   And sold to slavery, of my redemption[112] thence,
And portance[113] in my travels' history;
Wherein of antres[114] vast and deserts idle,
Rough quarries, rocks, and hills whose heads touch heaven,

155   It was my hint to speak,— such was the process;
And of the Cannibals that each other eat,
The Anthropophagi, and men whose heads
Do grow beneath their shoulders. This to hear
Would Desdemona seriously incline;

160   But still the house affairs would draw her thence,
Which ever as she could with haste dispatch,[115]
She'd come again, and with a greedy ear
Devour up my discourse; which I observing,
Took once a pliant[116] hour, and found good means

165   To draw from her a prayer of earnest heart
That I would all my pilgrimage dilate,[117]
Whereof by parcels[118] she had something heard,
But not intentively.[119] I did consent,
And often did beguile[120] her of her tears

170   When I did speak of some distressful stroke
That my youth suffer'd. My story being done,
She gave me for my pains a world of sighs;
She swore, in faith, 'twas strange, 'twas passing strange;
'Twas pitiful, 'twas wondrous pitiful. *Only worm*

175   She wish'd she had not heard it, yet she wish'd
That heaven had made her such a man; she thank'd me,
And bade me, if I had a friend that loved her,
I should but teach him how to tell my story,
And that would woo her. Upon this hint I spake:

180   She loved me for the dangers I had pass'd,
And I loved her that she did pity them.
This only is the witchcraft I have used.
Here comes the lady; let her witness it.

Enter Desdemona, Iago, and the rest.

DUKE: I think this tale would win my daughter too.

Good Brabantio,
185   Take up this mangled matter at the best:
Men do their broken weapons rather use
Than their bare hands.
BRAB: I pray you, hear her speak:
If she confess that she was half the wooer,
190   Destruction on my head, if my bad blame
Light on the man! Come hither, gentle mistress:
Do you perceive in all this noble company
Where most you owe obedience?
DESD: My noble father,
195   I do perceive here a divided duty.
To you I am bound for life and education;
My life and education both do learn me
How to respect you; you are the lord of duty,
I am hitherto your daughter. But here's my husband,
200   And so much duty as my mother show'd
To you, preferring you before her father,
So much I challenge that I may profess
Due to the Moor, my lord.
BRAB: God be with you! I have done.   *Məj*
205   Please it your Grace, on to the state affairs;
I had rather to adopt a child than get it.
Come hither, Moor:
I here do give thee that with all my heart
Which, but thou hast already, with all my heart
210   I would keep from thee. For your sake, jewel,
I am glad at soul I have no other child;
For thy escape would teach me tyranny,
To hang clogs[121] on them. I have done, my lord.
DUKE: Let me speak like yourself, and lay a sentence
215   Which, as a grise or step, may help these lovers
Into your favor.
When remedies are past, the griefs are ended[122]
By seeing the worst, which late on hopes depended.
To mourn a mischief that is past and gone
220   Is the next way to draw new mischief on.
What cannot be preserved when fortune takes,
Patience her injury a mockery makes.
The robb'd that smiles steals something from the thief;

[121]*weighted shackles*

[122]*Here the Duke begins a series of rhyming proverbs, which Brabantio will mock in the next lines.*

[123]*useless*

He robs himself that spends a bootless[123] grief.

225 BRAB: So let the Turk of Cyprus us beguile;

We lose it not so long as we can smile.

He bears the sentence well, that nothing bears

But the free comfort which from thence he hears;

But he bears both the sentence and the sorrow

230 That, to pay grief, must of poor patience borrow.

These sentences, to sugar or to gall,

Being strong on both sides, are equivocal.

But words are words; I never yet did hear

That the bruised heart was pierced through the ear.

235 I humbly beseech you, proceed to the affairs of state.

[124]*military defense*

[125]*acknowledged*

[126]*royal*

DUKE: The Turk with a most mighty preparation makes for

Cyprus. Othello, the fortitude[124] of the place is best known

to you; and though we have there a substitute of most

allowed[125] sufficiency, yet opinion, a sovereign[126] mistress

240 of effects, throws a more safer voice on you. You must

[127]*dirty*

therefore be content to slubber[127] the gloss of your new

fortunes with this more stubborn and boisterous expedi-

tion.

OTHELLO: The tyrant custom, most grave senators,

245 Hath made the flinty and steel couch of war

[128]*recognize*

My thrice driven bed of down. I do agnize[128]

A natural and prompt alacrity

[129]*difficult circum-
stances*

I find in hardness;[129] and do undertake

These present wars against the Ottomites.

250 Most humbly therefore bending to your state,

[130]*arrangements*

I crave fit disposition[130] for my wife,

[131]*lodging*

Due reference of place[131] and exhibition,[132]

[132]*financial allow-
ance*

With such accommodation and besort[133]

As levels with[134] her breeding.

[133]*company*

255 DUKE: If you please,

Be't at her father's.

[134]*suits*

BRAB: I'll not have it so.

OTHELLO: Nor I.

DESD: Nor I. I would not there reside

260 To put my father in impatient thoughts

By being in his eye. Most gracious Duke,

To my unfolding lend your prosperous ear.

DUKE: What would you, Desdemona?

DESD: That I did love the Moor to live with him,
265   My downright[135] violence and storm of fortunes

> [135]deliberate

May trumpet to the world. My heart's subdued
Even to the very quality of my lord:
I saw Othello's visage in his mind,
And to his honors and his valiant parts
270   Did I my soul and fortunes consecrate.
So that, dear lords, if I be left behind,
A moth of peace, and he go to the war,
The rites for which I love him are bereft[136] me,

> [136]taken from

And I a heavy interim[137] shall support

> [137]waiting period

275   By his dear absence. Let me go with him.
OTHELLO: Let her have your voices.[138]

> [138]support

    Vouch with me, heaven, I therefore beg it not
    To please the palate of my appetite;
    Nor to comply with heat[139] the young affects

> [139]sexual desires

280   In me defunct—and proper satisfaction;
    But to be free and bounteous to her mind;
    And heaven defend your good souls, that you think
    I will your serious and great business scant
    For[140] she is with me. No, when lightwing'd toys

> [140]because

285   Of feather'd Cupid seel[141] with wanton dullness

> [141]close up, blind

    My speculative and officed instruments,[142]

> [142]intellectual ability and official duties

    That my disports[143] corrupt and taint my business,

> [143]entertainment

    Let housewives make a skillet of my helm,
    And all indign[144] and base adversities

> [144]undeserving

290   Make head[145] against my estimation![146]

> [145]headway
>
> [146]reputation

DUKE: Be it as you shall privately determine,
    Either for her stay or going: the affair cries haste,
    And speed must answer't: you must hence tonight.
DESD: Tonight, my lord?
295 DUKE: This night.
OTHELLO: With all my heart.
DUKE: At nine i' the morning here we'll meet again.
    Othello, leave some officer behind,
    And he shall our commission bring to you;
300   With such things else of quality and respect
    As doth import you.
OTHELLO: So please your Grace, my ancient;
    A man he is of honesty and trust.

To his conveyance I assign my wife,
305   With what else needful your good Grace shall think
To be sent after me.
DUKE: Let it be so.
Good night to everyone.
And, noble signior,
310   If virtue no delighted beauty lack,
Your son-in-law is far more fair than black.
FIRST SENATOR: Adieu, brave Moor, use Desdemona well.
BRAB: Look to her, Moor, if thou hast eyes to see:
She has deceived her father, and may thee.
315   *Exeunt [Duke, Senators, and Officers.]*
OTHELLO: My life upon her faith! Honest Iago,
My Desdemona must I leave to thee:
I prithee, let thy wife attend on her;
And bring them after in the best advantage.
Come, Desdemona, I have but an hour

147*domestic*   320   Of love, of worldly[147] matters and direction,
To spend with thee: We must obey the time.
         [Exeunt [Othello] and Desdemona.]
ROD: Iago!
IAGO: What say'st thou, noble heart?
ROD: What will I do, thinkest thou?
325   IAGO: Why, go to bed and sleep.

148*immediately*   ROD: I will incontinently[148] drown myself.
IAGO: If thou dost, I shall never love thee after.
Why, thou silly gentleman!
ROD: It is silliness to live when to live is torment, and then
330   have we a prescription to die when death is our physician.
IAGO: O villainous! I have looked upon the world for four
times seven years, and since I could distinguish betwixt a
benefit and an injury, I never found man that knew how
to love himself. Ere I would say I would drown myself for

149*insignificant*   335   the love of a guinea hen,[149] I would change my humanity
woman   with a baboon.
ROD: What should I do? I confess it is my shame to be so
fond, but it is not in my virtue to amend it.
IAGO: Virtue? a fig! 'Tis in ourselves that we are thus or
340   thus. Our bodies are gardens, to the which our wills are
gardeners; so that if we will plant nettles or sow lettuce,

set hyssop and weed up thyme, supply it with one gender of
herbs or distract it with many, either to have it sterile with
idleness or manured with industry, why, the power and
345 corrigible authority[150] of this lies in our wills. If the balance
of our lives had not one scale of reason to poise[151] another
of sensuality, the blood and baseness of our natures would
conduct us to most preposterous conclusions. But we have
reason to cool our raging motions, our carnal stings, our
350 unbitted lusts.

ROD: It cannot be.

IAGO: It is merely a lust of the blood and a permission of the
will. Come, be a man! Drown thyself? Drown cats and blind
puppies! I have professed me thy friend, and I confess me
355 knit to thy deserving with cables of perdurable[152] toughness;
I could never better stead[153] thee than now. Put money in
thy purse; follow thou the wars; defeat thy favor with an
usurped beard. I say, put money in thy purse. It cannot
be that Desdemona should long continue her love to the
360 Moor—put money in thy purse—nor he his to her. It was a
violent commencement,[154] and thou shalt see an answerable
sequestration;[155] put but money in thy purse. These Moors
are changeable in their wills:—fill thy purse with money.
The food that to him now is as luscious as locusts, shall
365 be to him shortly as acerb[156] as the coloquintida.[157] She must
change[158] for youth; when she is sated with his body, she
will find the error of her choice. She must have change, she
must; therefore put money in thy purse. If thou wilt needs
damn thyself, do it a more delicate way than drowning.
370 Make all the money thou canst. If sanctimony and a frail
vow betwixt an erring barbarian and a supersubtle Venetian
be not too hard for my wits and all the tribe of hell, thou
shalt enjoy her; therefore make money. A pox of drowning
thyself! It is clean out of the way. Seek thou rather to be
375 hanged in compassing[159] thy joy than to be drowned and go
without her.

ROD: Wilt thou be fast to my hopes, if I depend on the issue?

IAGO: Thou art sure of me; go, make money. I have told thee
often, and I retell thee again and again, I hate the Moor.
380 My cause is hearted; thine hath no less reason. Let us be
conjunctive[160] in our revenge against him. If thou canst

---

[150]*ability to correct*

[151]*balance*

[152]*durable*

[153]*serve*

[154]*beginning*

[155]*divorce*

[156]*bitter*

[157]*drug made from a bitter gourd*

[158]*exchange Othello*

[159]*containing*

[160]*cooperative*

cuckold him, thou dost thyself a pleasure, me a sport.
There are many events in the womb of time which will be
delivered. Traverse, go, provide thy money. We will have
385   more of this tomorrow. Adieu.

ROD: Where shall we meet i' the morning?

IAGO: At my lodging.

ROD: I'll be with thee betimes.

IAGO: Go to, farewell. Do you hear, Roderigo?

390   ROD: What say you?

IAGO: No more of drowning, do you hear?

ROD: I am changed; I'll go sell all my land.   *[Exit Roderigo.]*

IAGO: Thus do I ever make my fool my purse;
    For I mine own gain'd knowledge should profane,[161]
395   If I would time expend with such a snipe[162]
    But for my sport and profit. I hate the Moor;
    And it is thought abroad that 'twixt my sheets
    He has done my office. I know not if't be true;
    But I for mere suspicion in that kind
400   Will do as if for surety.[163] He holds me well;
    The better shall my purpose work on him.
    Cassio's a proper man. Let me see now:
    To get his place, and to plume up my will
    In double knavery—How, how? —Let's see—
405   After some time, to abuse Othello's ear
    That he is too familiar with his wife.
    He hath a person and a smooth dispose[164]
    To be suspected; framed to make women false.
    The Moor is of a free and open nature,
410   That thinks men honest that but seem to be so;
    And will as tenderly be led by the nose
    As asses are.
    I have't. It is engender'd. Hell and night
    Must bring this monstrous birth to the world's light.

Exit.

[161] *violate*

[162] *dumb bird*

[163] *certainty*

[164] *appearance*

[ACT II]

[SCENE I]
[A seaport in Cyprus.]

[Enter Montano, govenor of Cyprus, and two other Gentlemen.]

MONTANO: What from the cape can you discern at sea?
FIRST GENTLEMAN: Nothing at all. It is a highwrought flood;
    I cannot, 'twixt the heaven and the main,
    Descry[1] a sail.
5 MONTANO: Methinks the wind hath spoke aloud at land;
    A fuller blast ne'er shook our battlements:
    If it hath ruffian'd[2] so upon the sea,
    What ribs of oak,[3] when mountains melt on them,
    Can hold the mortise?[4] What shall we hear of this?
10 SECOND GENTLEMAN: A segregation[5] of the Turkish fleet: For do
    but stand upon the foaming shore,
    The chidden[6] billow seems to pelt the clouds;
    The windshaked surge, with high and monstrous mane,
    Seems to cast water on the burning bear,[7]
15   And quench the guards[8] of the everfixed pole:
    I never did like molestation[9] view
    On the enchafed[10] flood.
  MONTANO: If that the Turkish fleet
    Be not enshelter'd and embay'd,[11] they are drown'd;
20   It is impossible to bear it out.

Enter a third Gentleman.

THIRD GENTLEMAN: News, lads! Our wars are done.
    The desperate tempest hath so bang'd the Turks,
    That their designment[12] halts: a noble ship of Venice

[1] *make out*

[2] *acted violent*

[3] *planks of a ship*

[4] *fastening joints*

[5] *breaking up*

[6] *punished*

[7] *Ursa Minor, a constellation in the shape of a bear*

[8] *stars near the North Star*

[9] *harassment*

[10] *upset*

[11] *harbored in a bay*

[12] *plan*

Hath seen a grievous wreck and sufferance

25   On most part of their fleet.

MONTANO: How? Is this true?

THIRD GENTLEMAN: The ship is here put in;

    A Veronesa, Michael Cassio,

    Lieutenant to the warlike Moor, Othello,

30   Is come on shore; the Moor himself at sea,

    And is in full commission[13] here for Cyprus.

MONTANO: I am glad on't; 'tis a worthy governor.

THIRD GENTLEMAN: But this same Cassio, though he speak
            of comfort

35   Touching the Turkish loss, yet he looks sadly

    And prays the Moor be safe; for they were parted

    With foul and violent tempest.

MONTANO: Pray heavens he be;

    For I have served him, and the man commands

40   Like a full soldier. Let's to the seaside, ho!

    As well to see the vessel that's come in

    As to throw out our eyes for brave Othello,

    Even till we make the main and the aerial blue

    An indistinct[14] regard.

45 THIRD GENTLEMAN: Come, let's do so;

    For every minute is expectancy

    Of more arrivance.

Enter Cassio.

CASSIO: Thanks, you the valiant of this warlike isle,

    That so approve the Moor! O, let the heavens

50   Give him defense against the elements,

    For I have lost him on a dangerous sea.

MONTANO: Is he well shipp'd?

CASSIO: His bark is stoutly timber'd, and his pilot

    Of very expert and approved allowance;

55   Therefore my hopes, not surfeited to death,[15]

    Stand in bold cure.[16]   *Enter a messenger.*

MESSENGER: A sail, a sail, a sail!

[13]*preparation*

[14]*inseparable*

[15]*overindulged*

[16]*chance of coming true*

Cassio: What noise?

Messenger: The town is empty; on the brow o' the sea
Stand ranks of people, and they cry, "A sail!"

60 Cassio: My hopes do shape him for the governor. *A shot.*

Second Gentleman: They do discharge their shot of courtesy: [17]
Our friends at least.

Cassio: I pray you, sir, go forth,
And give us truth who 'tis that is arrived.

65 Second Gentleman: I shall. *Exit.*

Montano: But, good lieutenant, is your general wived?

Cassio: Most fortunately: he hath achieved a maid
That paragons[18] description and wild fame;
One that excels the quirks[19] of blazoning pens,

70 And in the essential vesture[20] of creation
Does tire the ingener.[21]

Enter second Gentleman.
How now! who has put in?

Second Gentleman: 'Tis one Iago, ancient to the general.

Cassio: He has had most favorable and happy speed:
Tempests themselves, high seas, and howling winds,

75 The gutter'd[22] rocks, and congregated[23] sands,
Traitors ensteep'd to clog the guiltless keel,
As having sense of beauty, do omit
Their mortal natures, letting go safely by
The divine Desdemona.

80 Montano: What is she?

Cassio: She that I spake of, our great captain's captain,
Left in the conduct of the bold Iago;
Whose footing here anticipates our thoughts
A se'nnight's[24] speed. Great Jove,[25] Othello guard,

85 And swell his sail with thine own powerful breath,
That he may bless this bay with his tall ship,
Make love's quick pants in Desdemona's arms,
Give renew'd fire to our extincted spirits,
And bring all Cyprus comfort.

Enter Desdemona, Iago, Emilia, Roderigo.
90 O, behold,
The riches of the ship is come on shore!

[17]*greeting shot, meant to show friendship*

[18]*outdoes*

[19]*figures of speech*

[20]*clothing [i.e., her natural traits]*

[21]*one who might describe her*

[22]*jagged*

[23]*accumulated*

[24]*week's*

[25]*in Roman mythology, king of the gods*

²⁶*[He asked them to kneel.]*

Ye men of Cyprus, let her have your knees.²⁶
Hail to thee, lady! And the grace of heaven,
Before, behind thee, and on every hand,
95   Enwheel thee round!
DESD: I thank you, valiant Cassio.
What tidings can you tell me of my lord?
CASSIO: He is not yet arrived; nor know I aught
But that he's well and will be shortly here.
100 DESD: O, but I fear—How lost you company?

²⁷*argument*

CASSIO: The great contention²⁷ of the sea and skies
Parted our fellowship—But, hark! a sail.

Within: "A sail, a sail!"

SECOND GENTLEMAN: They give their greeting to the citadel:
This likewise is a friend.
105 CASSIO: See for the news.   *[Exit Gentleman.]*

²⁸*annoy*

Good ancient, you are welcome. Welcome, mistress.
Let it not gall²⁸ your patience, good Iago,
That I extend my manners; 'tis my breeding
That gives me this bold show of courtesy.
110 IAGO: Sir, would she give you so much of her lips
As of her tongue she oft bestows on me,
You'ld have enough.
DESD: Alas, she has no speech.
IAGO: In faith, too much;

²⁹*desire*

115   I find it still when I have list²⁹ to sleep:
Marry, before your ladyship, I grant
She puts her tongue a little in her heart
And chides with thinking.
EMILIA: You have little cause to say so.
120 IAGO: Come on, come on. You are pictures out of doors,
Bells in your parlors, wildcats in your kitchens,
Saints in your injuries, devils being offended,

³⁰*domestic affairs*

³¹*loose women*

Players in your housewifery,³⁰ and housewives³¹ in your
beds.
125 DESD: O, fie upon thee, slanderer!
IAGO: Nay, it is true, or else I am a Turk:
You rise to play, and go to bed to work.
EMILIA: You shall not write my praise.
IAGO: No, let me not.

130 **Desd:** What wouldst thou write of me, if thou shouldst praise
      me?
    Iago: O gentle lady, do not put me to't;
      For I am nothing if not critical.
    Desd: Come on, assay³²—There's one gone to the harbor?   ³²*try*
135 **Iago:** Ay, madam.
    Desd: I am not merry, but I do beguile³³   ³³*trick*
      The thing I am by seeming otherwise.
      Come, how wouldst thou praise me?
    Iago: I am about it; but indeed my invention
140   Comes from my pate as birdlime³⁴ does from frieze;³⁵   ³⁴*sticky substance*
      It plucks out brains and all. But my Muse labors,   ³⁵*coarse cloth*
      And thus she is deliver'd.
      If she be fair and wise, fairness and wit,
      The one's for use, the other useth it.
145 **Desd:** Well praised! How if she be black and witty?
    Iago: If she be black, and thereto³⁶ have a wit,   ³⁶*also*
      She'll find a white that shall her blackness fit.
    Desd: Worse and worse.
    Emilia: How if fair and foolish?
150 **Iago:** She never yet was foolish that was fair;
      For even her folly help'd her to an heir.
    Desd: These are old fond paradoxes to make fools laugh i' the
      alehouse. What miserable praise hast thou for her that's
      foul and foolish?
155 **Iago:** There's none so foul and foolish thereunto,
      But does foul pranks which fair and wise ones do.
    Desd: O heavy ignorance! Thou praisest the worst best. But
      what praise couldst thou bestow on a deserving woman
      indeed, one that in the authority of her merit did justly put
160   on the vouch³⁷ of very malice itself?   ³⁷*approval*
    Iago: She that was ever fair and never proud,
      Had tongue at will and yet was never loud,
      Never lack'd gold and yet went never gay,
      Fled from her wish and yet said, "Now I may";
165   She that, being anger'd, her revenge being nigh,
      Bade her wrong stay and her displeasure fly;
      She that in wisdom never was so frail
      To change the cod's head for the salmon's tail;³⁸   ³⁸*i.e., trade one useless thing for another*
      She that could think and ne'er disclose her mind,

39person

40nurse babies and
keep household
accounts [that is,
do unimportant
tasks]

41free-speaking

42plainly

43shackle

44gentleman

45enema tubes

46ship

47follows

170   See suitors following and not look behind;
       She was a wight,39 if ever such wight were—
DESD: To do what?
IAGO: To suckle fools and chronicle small beer.40
DESD: O most lame and impotent conclusion! Do not learn
175   of him, Emilia, though he be thy husband. How say you,
       Cassio? Is he not a most profane and liberal41 counselor?
CASSIO: He speaks home,42 madam. You may relish him more
       in the soldier than in the scholar.
IAGO: [Aside.] He takes her by the palm; ay, well said, whis-
180   per. With as little a web as this will I ensnare as great a
       fly as Cassio. Ay, smile upon her, do; I will gyve43 thee
       in thine own courtship. You say true; 'tis so, indeed. If
       such tricks as these strip you out of your lieutenantry,
       it had been better you had not kissed your three fingers
185   so oft, which now again you are most apt to play the sir44
       in. Very good. Well kissed! an excellent courtesy! 'tis so,
       indeed. Yet again your fingers to your lips? Would they
       were clysterpipes45 for your sake! (Trumpets without.) The
       Moor! I know his trumpet.
190 CASSIO: 'Tis truly so.
DESD: Let's meet him and receive him.
CASSIO: Lo, where he comes!

Enter Othello and Attendants.

OTHELLO: O my fair warrior!
DESD: My dear Othello!
195 OTHELLO: It gives me wonder great as my content
       To see you here before me. O my soul's joy!
       If after every tempest come such calms,
       May the winds blow till they have waken'd death!
       And let the laboring bark46 climb hills of seas
200   Olympus high, and duck again as low
       As hell's from heaven! If it were now to die,
       'Twere now to be most happy; for I fear
       My soul hath her content so absolute
       That not another comfort like to this
205   Succeeds47 in unknown fate.
DESD: The heavens forbid

But that our loves and comforts should increase,
Even as our days do grow!

OTHELLO: Amen to that, sweet powers!
210   I cannot speak enough of this content;
It stops me here; it is too much of joy:
And this, and this,[48] the greatest discords be   *They kiss.*   [48]*these kisses*
That e'er our hearts shall make!

IAGO: O, you are well tuned now!
215   But I'll set down[49] the pegs that make this music,   [49]*unscrew*
As honest as I am.

OTHELLO: Come, let us to the castle.
News, friends: our wars are done, the Turks are drown'd.
Honey, you shall be well desired in Cyprus;
220   I have found great love amongst them. O my sweet,
I prattle[50] out of fashion, and I dote   [50]*chatter*
In mine own comforts. I prithee, good Iago,
Go to the bay and disembark my coffers:[51]   [51]*treasure chests*
Bring thou the master to the citadel;
225   He is a good one, and his worthiness
Does challenge much respect. Come, Desdemona,
Once more well met at Cyprus.

Exit Othello and Desdemona.

IAGO: Do thou meet me presently at the harbor. Come hither.
If thou be'st valiant—as they say base men being in love
230   have then a nobility in their natures more than is native to
them—list me. The lieutenant tonight watches on the court
of guard. First, I must tell thee this: Desdemona is directly[52]   [52]*certainly*
in love with him.

ROD: With him? Why, 'tis not possible.

235   IAGO: Lay thy finger thus,[53] and let thy soul be instructed. Mark   [53]*[He puts a finger*
me with what violence she first loved the Moor, but for   *to his lips.]*
bragging and telling her fantastical lies. And will she love
him still for prating?[54] Let not thy discreet heart think it.   [54]*babbling*
Her eye must be fed; and what delight shall she have to look
240   on the devil? When the blood is made dull with the act of
sport, there should be, again to inflame it and to give sati-
ety a fresh appetite, loveliness in favor, sympathy in years,
manners, and beauties; all which the Moor is defective in.
Now, for want of these required conveniences, her deli-
245   cate tenderness will find itself abused, begin to heave the

[55] make her feel sick

[56] obvious

[57] having a conscience

[58] obscene

[59] requirements

250 gorge,[55] disrelish and abhor the Moor; very nature will instruct her in it and compel her to some second choice. Now sir, this granted—as it is a most pregnant[56] and unforced position—who stands so eminently in the degree of this fortune as Cassio does? A knave very voluble; no further conscionable[57] than in putting on the mere form of civil and humane seeming, for the better compassing of his salt[58] and most hidden loose affection? Why, none; why, none; a slipper and subtle knave, a finder out

255 of occasions; that has an eye can stamp and counterfeit advantages, though true advantage never present itself: a devilish knave! Besides, the knave is handsome, young, and hath all those requisites[59] in him that folly and green minds look after; a pestilent complete knave; and the

260 woman hath found him already.

ROD: I cannot believe that in her; she's full of most blest condition.

IAGO: Blest fig'send! The wine she drinks is made of grapes. If she had been blest, she would never have loved the

265 Moor. Blest pudding! Didst thou not see her paddle with the palm of his hand? Didst not mark that?

ROD: Yes, that I did; but that was but courtesy.

IAGO: Lechery, by this hand; an index and obscure prologue to the history of lust and foul thoughts. They met so

270 near with their lips that their breaths embraced together. Villainous thoughts, Roderigo! When these mutualities[60] so marshal the way, hard at hand comes the master and main exercise, the incorporate[61] conclusion. Pish! But,

[60] expressions of love between two people

[61] bringing two bodies together [resulting in sexual intercourse]

[62] undermining

sir, be you ruled by me. I have brought you from Venice.

275 Watch you tonight; for the command, I'll lay't upon you. Cassio knows you not. I'll not be far from you. Do you find some occasion to anger Cassio, either by speaking too loud, or tainting[62] his discipline, or from what other course you please, which the time shall more favorably

280 minister.

ROD: Well.

IAGO: Sir, he is rash and very sudden in choler, and haply may strike at you. Provoke him, that he may; for even out of that will I cause these of Cyprus to mutiny, whose

[63] satisfaction

285 qualification[63] shall come into no true taste again but by the displanting of Cassio. So shall you have a shorter jour-

ney to your desires by the means I shall then have to prefer[64]
them, and the impediment most profitably removed, without the which there were no expectation of our prosperity.

290   ROD: I will do this, if I can bring it to any opportunity.

IAGO: I warrant thee. Meet me by and by at the citadel. I must
fetch his necessaries ashore. Farewell.

ROD: Adieu.   *Exit.*

IAGO: That Cassio loves her, I do well believe it;
295   That she loves him, 'tis apt and of great credit:[65]
The Moor, howbeit that I endure him not,
Is of a constant, loving, noble nature;
And I dare think he'll prove to Desdemona
A most dear husband. Now, I do love her too,
300   Not out of absolute lust, though peradventure
I stand accountant[66] for as great a sin,
But partly led to diet[67] my revenge,
For that I do suspect the lusty Moor
Hath leap'd into my seat; the thought whereof
305   Doth like a poisonous mineral gnaw my inwards,[68]
And nothing can or shall content my soul
Till I am even'd with him, wife for wife;
Or failing so, yet that I put the Moor
At least into a jealousy so strong
310   That judgement cannot cure. Which thing to do,
If this poor trash of Venice, whom I trash[69]
For his quick hunting,[70] stand the putting on,[71]
I'll have our Michael Cassio on the hip,[72]
Abuse him to the Moor in the rank garb:
315   For I fear Cassio with my nightcap too;[73]
Make the Moor thank me, love me, and reward me,
For making him egregiously[74] an ass
And practicing upon his peace and quiet
Even to madness. 'Tis here, but yet confused:
320   Knavery's plain face is never seen till used.

Exit.

[64]*favor*

[65]*likely and believable*

[66]*accountable*

[67]*feed*

[68]*insides*

[69]*restrain [a hunting term]*

[70]*in order to make him hunt*

[71]*takes the bait*

[72]*at my bidding*

[73]*i.e. in my bed*

[74]*conspicuously*

[SCENE II]
[A street.]

Enter a Gentleman reading a proclamation.

HERALD: It is Othello's pleasure, our noble and valiant
    general, that upon certain tidings[75] now arrived, import-
    ing[76] the mere[77] perdition[78] of the Turkish fleet, every man
    put himself into triumph; some to dance, some to make
5   bonfires, each man to what sport and revels his addiction
    leads him; for besides these beneficial news, it is the cel-
    ebration of his nuptial. So much was his pleasure should
    be proclaimed. All offices are open, and there is full lib-
    erty of feasting from this present hour of five till the bell
10 have told eleven. Heaven bless the isle of Cyprus and our
    noble general Othello!

                                                        Exit.

[SCENE III]
[A hall in the castle.]

Enter Othello, Cassio, Desdemona, [and Attendants.]

OTHELLO: Good Michael, look you to the guard tonight:
    Let's teach ourselves that honorable stop,
    Not to outsport[79] discretion.
CASSIO: Iago hath direction what to do;
5   But notwithstanding,[80] with my personal eye
    Will I look to't.
OTHELLO: Iago is most honest.
    Michael, good night. Tomorrow with your earliest
    Let me have speech with you. Come, my dear love,
10 The purchase made, the fruits are to ensue;
    That profit's yet to come 'tween me and you.
    Good night.   *Exit Othello and Desdemona.*

Enter Iago.

[75]*news*

[76]*telling of*

[77]*total*

[78]*destruction*

[79]*make merry
beyond*

[80]*nevertheless,
anyway*

CASSIO: Welcome, Iago; we must to the watch.

IAGO: Not this hour, lieutenant; 'tis not yet ten o' the clock. Our
15   general cast us thus early for the love of his Desdemona;
     who let us not therefore blame. He hath not yet made wan-
     ton the night with her, and she is sport for Jove.[81]

CASSIO: She's a most exquisite lady.

IAGO: And, I'll warrant her, full of game.

20 CASSIO: Indeed she's a most fresh and delicate creature.

IAGO: What an eye she has!
     Methinks it sounds a parley[82] to provocation.

CASSIO: An inviting eye; and yet methinks right modest.

IAGO: And when she speaks, is it not an alarum to love?

25 CASSIO: She is indeed perfection.

IAGO: Well, happiness to their sheets! Come, lieutenant, I have
     a stoup[83] of wine, and here without are a brace of Cyprus
     gallants that would fain have a measure to the health of
     black Othello.

30 CASSIO: Not tonight, good Iago: I have very poor and unhappy
     brains for drinking. I could well wish courtesy would
     invent some other custom of entertainment.

IAGO: O, they are our friends! But one cup; I'll drink for you.

CASSIO: I have drunk but one cup tonight, and that was craftily
35   qualified[84] too, and behold what innovation[85] it makes here.
     I am unfortunate in the infirmity, and dare not task[86] my
     weakness with any more.

IAGO: What, man! 'Tis a night of revels, the gallants desire it.

CASSIO: Where are they?

40 IAGO: Here at the door; I pray you, call them in.

CASSIO: I'll do't, but it dislikes me.   *Exit.*

IAGO: If I can fasten but one cup upon him,
     With that which he hath drunk tonight already,
     He'll be as full of quarrel and offense
45   As my young mistress' dog. Now my sick fool Roderigo,
     Whom love hath turn'd almost the wrong side out,
     To Desdemona hath tonight caroused
     Potations pottledeep;[87] and he's to watch:
     Three lads of Cyprus, noble swelling spirits,
50   That hold their honors in a wary distance,[88]
     The very elements of this warlike isle,
     Have I tonight fluster'd with flowing cups,

[81] *[The king of the gods was famous for sexual exploits.]*

[82] *inviting call [a military term]*

[83] *two-quart container*

[84] *diluted*

[85] *change*

[86] *test*

[87] *potfuls of alcohol*

[88] *i.e., They consider honor a very sensitive subject.*

And they watch too. Now, 'mongst this flock of
    drunkards,
55   Am I to put our Cassio in some action[89]
That may offend the isle. But here they come:
If consequence[90] do but approve[91] my dream,[92]
My boat sails freely, both with wind and stream.

[Enter Montano, Cassio and others [Gentlemen.]]

CASSIO: 'Fore God, they have given me a rouse already.
60   MONTANO: Good faith, a little one; not past a pint, as I am a
    soldier.
IAGO: Some wine, ho!

[Sings.]   "And let me the canakin clink, clink;
                And let me the canakin clink:
65   A soldier's a man;
                O, man's life's but a span;
                Why then let a soldier drink."

Some wine, boys!
CASSIO: 'Fore God, an excellent song.
70   IAGO: I learned it in England, where indeed they are most
    potent in potting. Your Dane, your German, and your
    swagbellied Hollander—Drink, ho!—are nothing to your
    English.
CASSIO: Is your Englishman so expert in his drinking?
75   IAGO: Why, he drinks you with facility your Dane dead
    drunk; he sweats not to overthrow your Almain; he gives
    your Hollander a vomit ere the next pottle can be filled.
CASSIO: To the health of our general!
MONTANO: I am for it, lieutenant, and I'll do you justice.
80   IAGO: O sweet England!
[Sings.]   "King Stephen was a worthy peer,
                His breeches cost him but a crown;
                He held them sixpence all too dear,
                With that he call'd the tailor lown.
85   "He was a wight of high renown,
                And thou art but of low degree:

[89] situation

[90] what happens
after this

[91] prove true

[92] vision of things

'Tis pride that pulls the country down;
  Then take thine auld cloak about thee."

Some wine, ho!

90 CASSIO: Why, this is a more exquisite song than the other.

IAGO: Will you hear't again?

CASSIO: No, for I hold him to be unworthy of his place that
  does those things. Well, God's above all, and there be souls
  must be saved, and there be souls must not be saved.

95 IAGO: It's true, good lieutenant.

CASSIO: For mine own part—no offense to the general, nor any
  man of quality—I hope to be saved.

IAGO: And so do I too, lieutenant.

CASSIO: Ay, but, by your leave, not before me; the lieutenant is
100   to be saved before the ancient. Let's have no more of this;
  let's to our affairs. God forgive us our sins! Gentlemen, let's
  look to our business. Do not think, gentlemen, I am drunk:
  this is my ancient, this is my right hand, and this is my left.
  I am not drunk now; I can stand well enough, and I speak
105   well enough.

ALL: Excellent well.

CASSIO: Why, very well then; you must not think then that I am
  drunk.   *Exit.*

MONTANO: To the platform, masters; come, let's set the watch.

110 IAGO: You see this fellow that is gone before;
  He is a soldier fit to stand by Caesar
  And give direction. And do but see his vice;
  'Tis to his virtue a just equinox,
  The one as long as the other. 'Tis pity of him.

115 I fear the trust Othello puts him in
  On some odd time of his infirmity
  Will shake this island.

MONTANO: But is he often thus?

IAGO: 'Tis evermore the prologue to his sleep;

120 He'll watch the horologe[93] a double set,
  If drink rock not his cradle.

MONTANO: It were well
  The general were put in mind of it.
  Perhaps he sees it not, or his good nature

125 Prizes the virtue that appears in Cassio
  And looks not on his evils: Is not this true?

[93]*clock*

Enter Roderigo.

IAGO: How now, Roderigo!
    I pray you, after the lieutenant; go.   *Exit Roderigo.*
MONTANO: And 'tis great pity that the noble Moor
130   Should hazard such a place as his own second
    With one of an ingraft[94] infirmity:
    It were an honest action to say
    So to the Moor.
IAGO: Not I, for this fair island:
135   I do love Cassio well, and would do much
    To cure him of this evil:—But, hark! What noise?
                     (Without:) "Help, help!"

Enter Cassio, driving in Roderigo.

CASSIO: 'Zounds! You rogue! You rascal!
MONTANO: What's the matter, lieutenant?
CASSIO: A knave teach me my duty! But I'll beat the knave
140   into a twiggen[95] bottle.
ROD: Beat me!
CASSIO: Dost thou prate, rogue?   *Strikes Roderigo.*
MONTANO: Nay, good lieutenant; I pray you, sir, hold your
          hand.
145 CASSIO: Let me go, sir, or I'll knock you o'er the mazzard.[96]
MONTANO: Come, come, you're drunk.
CASSIO: Drunk!   *They*
    fight.
IAGO: Away, I say; go out and cry a mutiny.
150   *[Exit Roderigo.]*
    Nay, good lieutenant! God's will, gentlemen!
    Help, ho!—Lieutenant—sir—Montano sir—
    Help, masters! Here's a goodly watch indeed! *(A bell*
    rings.) Who's that that rings the bell?—Diablo, ho!
155   The town will rise. God's will, lieutenant, hold!
    You will be shamed forever.

Enter Othello, and Gentlemen with weapons.

OTHELLO: What is the matter here?
MONTANO: 'Zounds, I bleed still; I am hurt to the death

[94]*native*

[95]*made of twigs*

[96]*head*

OTHELLO: Hold, for your lives!

IAGO: Hold, ho!—Lieutenant—sir—Montano—gentlemen—

160   Have you forgot all place of sense and duty?

     Hold! the general speaks to you! Hold, hold, for shame!

OTHELLO: Why, how now, ho! from whence ariseth this? Are

     we turn'd Turks, and to ourselves do that

     Which heaven hath forbid the Ottomites?

165   For Christian shame, put by[97] this barbarous brawl:

     He that stirs next to carve for his own rage

     Holds his soul light; he dies upon his motion.

     Silence that dreadful bell; it frights the isle

     From her propriety. What is the matter, masters?

170   Honest Iago, that look'st dead with grieving,

     Speak, who began this? On thy love, I charge thee:

IAGO: I do not know: Friends all but now, even now,

     In quarter,[98] and in terms like bride and groom

     Devesting them for bed;[99] and then, but now

175   As if some planet had unwitted men,

     Swords out, and tilting one at other's breast,

     In opposition bloody. I cannot speak

     Any beginning to this peevish odds.

OTHELLO: How comes it, Michael, you are thus forgot?

180 CASSIO: I pray you, pardon me; I cannot speak.

OTHELLO: Worthy Montano, you were wont[100] be civil;

     The gravity and stillness of your youth

     The world hath noted, and your name is great

     In mouths of wisest censure. What's the matter,

185   That you unlace your reputation thus,

     And spend[101] your rich opinion for the name

     Of a nightbrawler? Give me answer to it.

MONTANO: Worthy Othello, I am hurt to danger:

     Your officer, Iago, can inform you—

190   While I spare speech, which something now offends[102] me—

     Of all that I do know. Nor know I aught

     By me that's said or done amiss this night;

     Unless self-charity be sometimes a vice,

     And to defend ourselves it be a sin

195   When violence assails us.

OTHELLO: Now, by heaven,

     My blood begins my safer guides to rule,

     And passion, having my best judgement collied,[103]

[97]*cease*

[98]*relationship*

[99]*i.e., speaking to one another as sweetly as a married couple getting ready for bed*

[100]*accustomed [to]*

[101]*trade*

[102]*hurts*

[103]*darkened; muddied*

Assays to lead the way. If I once stir,
200   Or do but lift this arm, the best of you
Shall sink in my rebuke. Give me to know
How this foul rout began, who set it on,
And he that is approved[104] in this offense,
Though he had twinn'd with me, both at a birth,
205   Shall lose me. What! in a town of war,
Yet wild, the people's hearts brimful of fear,
To manage[105] private and domestic quarrel,
In night, and on the court and guard of safety![106]
'Tis monstrous. Iago, who began't?

210 MONTANO: If partially affined,[107] or leagued in office,[108]
Thou dost deliver more or less than truth,
Thou art no soldier.

IAGO: Touch me not so near:
I had rather have this tongue cut from my mouth
215   Than it should do offense to Michael Cassio;
Yet, I persuade myself, to speak the truth
Shall nothing wrong him. Thus it is, general.
Montano and myself being in speech,
There comes a fellow crying out for help,
220   And Cassio following him with determined sword,
To execute upon him. Sir, this gentleman
Steps in to Cassio and entreats his pause:
Myself the crying fellow did pursue,
Lest by his clamor—as it so fell out—
225   The town might fall in fright. He, swift of foot,
Outran my purpose; and I return'd the rather
For that I heard the clink and fall of swords,
And Cassio high in oath, which till tonight
I ne'er might say before. When I came back—
230   For this was brief —I found them close together,
At blow and thrust, even as again they were
When you yourself did part them.
More of this matter cannot I report.
But men are men; the best sometimes forget:
235   Though Cassio did some little wrong to him,
As men in rage strike those that wish them best,
Yet surely Cassio, I believe, received
From him that fled some strange indignity,
Which patience could not pass.[109]

[104]*found guilty*

[105]*carry out*

[106]*your official watch*

[107]*biased by friendship*

[108]*influenced by your official relationship*

[109]*allow*

OTHELLO: I know, Iago,
240 Thy honesty and love doth mince[110] this matter,
  Making it light to Cassio. Cassio, I love thee;
  But never more be officer of mine.

Enter Desdemona with others.
  Look, if my gentle love be not raised up!
  I'll make thee an example.
245 DESD: What's the matter?
OTHELLO: All's well now, sweeting; come away to bed.
  Sir, for your hurts, myself will be your surgeon.
  Lead him off.

      [To Montano who is led off.]
  Iago, look with care about the town,
250 And silence those whom this vile brawl distracted.
  Come, Desdemona, 'tis the soldiers' life—
  To have their balmy slumbers waked with strife.

   Exit Moor [Othello], Desdemona, Attendants.
IAGO: What, are you hurt, lieutenant?
CASSIO: Ay, past all surgery.
255 IAGO: Marry, heaven forbid!
CASSIO: Reputation, reputation, reputation! O, I have lost my
  reputation! I have lost the immortal part of myself, and what
  remains is bestial. My reputation, Iago, my reputation!
IAGO: As I am an honest man, I thought you had received some
260 bodily wound; there is more sense in that than in reputation. Reputation is an idle and most false imposition; oft
  got without merit and lost without deserving. You have
  lost no reputation at all, unless you repute yourself such
  a loser. What, man! there are ways to recover the general
265 again. You are but now cast in his mood, a punishment
  more in policy than in malice; even so as one would beat
  his offenseless dog to affright an imperious lion. Sue to him
  again, and he's yours.
CASSIO: I will rather sue to be despised than to deceive so good
270 a commander with so slight, so drunken, and so indiscreet
  an officer. Drunk? and speak parrot?[111] and squabble? swag-
  ger? swear? and discourse fustian[112] with one's own shadow?
  O thou invisible spirit of wine, if thou hast no name to be
  known by, let us call thee devil!
275 IAGO: What was he that you followed with your sword? What
  had he done to you?

[110]*make small, make light of*

[111]*nonsense*

[112]*rantingly*

CASSIO: I know not.

IAGO: Is't possible?

CASSIO: I remember a mass of things, but nothing distinctly;
280   a quarrel, but nothing wherefore. O God, that men should
      put an enemy in their mouths to steal away their brains!
      that we should, with joy, pleasance, revel, and applause,
      transform ourselves into beasts!

IAGO: Why, but you are now well enough. How came you
285   thus recovered?

CASSIO: It hath pleased the devil drunkenness to give place to
      the devil wrath: one unperfectness shows me another, to
      make me frankly despise myself.

IAGO: Come, you are too severe a moraler. As the time, the
290   place, and the condition of this country stands, I could
      heartily wish this had not befallen; but since it is as it is,
      mend it for your own good.

CASSIO: I will ask him for my place again; he shall tell me I
      am a drunkard! Had I as many mouths as Hydra,[113] such
295   an answer would stop them all. To be now a sensible man,
      by and by a fool, and presently a beast! O strange! Every
      inordinate[114] cup is unblest, and the ingredient is a devil.

IAGO: Come, come, good wine is a good familiar creature, if
      it be well used. Exclaim no more against it. And, good
300   lieutenant, I think you think I love you.

CASSIO: I have well approved it, sir. I drunk!

IAGO: You or any man living may be drunk at some time,
      man. I'll tell you what you shall do. Our general's wife is
      now the general. I may say so in this respect, for that he
305   hath devoted and given up himself to the contemplation,
      mark, and denotement of her parts and graces. Confess
      yourself freely to her; importune her help to put you
      in your place again. She is of so free, so kind, so apt, so
      blessed a disposition, she holds it a vice in her goodness
310   not to do more than she is requested. This broken joint
      between you and her husband entreat her to splinter;[115]
      and, my fortunes against any lay worth naming, this crack
      of your love shall grow stronger than it was before.

CASSIO: You advise me well.

315 IAGO: I protest, in the sincerity of love and honest kindness.

CASSIO: I think it freely; and betimes in the morning I will
      beseech the virtuous Desdemona to undertake for me. I

[113] a mythological beast said to have many heads

[114] excessive

[115] mend [as if with a splint]

am desperate of my fortunes if they[116] check[117] me here.

IAGO: You are in the right. Good night, lieutenant, I must to
320   the watch.

CASSIO: Good night, honest Iago.   *Exit.*

IAGO: And what's he then that says I play the villain?
     When this advice is free I give and honest,
     Probal[118] to thinking, and indeed the course
325   To win the Moor again? For 'tis most easy
     The inclining Desdemona to subdue
     In any honest suit. She's framed[119] as fruitful[120]
     As the free elements. And then for her
     To win the Moor, were't to renounce his baptism,
330   All seals and symbols of redeemed sin,
     His soul is so enfetter'd[121] to her love,
     That she may make, unmake, do what she list,
     Even as her appetite shall play the god
     With his weak function. How am I then a villain
335   To counsel Cassio to this parallel course,
     Directly to his good? Divinity of hell!
     When devils will the blackest sins put on,
     They do suggest at first with heavenly shows,
     As I do now. For whiles this honest fool
340   Plies Desdemona to repair his fortune,
     And she for him pleads strongly to the Moor,
     I'll pour this pestilence into his ear,
     That she repeals him for her body's lust;
     And by how much she strives to do him good,
345   She shall undo her credit with the Moor.
     So will I turn her virtue into pitch,[122]
     And out of her own goodness make the net
     That shall enmesh them all.

Enter Roderigo.
     How now, Roderigo!
350 ROD: I do follow here in the chase, not like a hound that hunts,
     but one that fills up the cry.[123] My money is almost spent; I
     have been tonight exceedingly well cudgeled;[124] and I think
     the issue will be, I shall have so much experience for my
     pains; and so, with no money at all and a little more wit,
355   return again to Venice.

IAGO: How poor are they that have not patience!

---

[116] *my fortunes*

[117] *stop*

[118] *likely; reasonable*

[119] *made*

[120] *generous*

[121] *enslaved [literally, "in chains"]*

[122] *a sticky trap*

[123] *not a lead hound, but one in the back of the pack*

[124] *beaten*

What wound did ever heal but by degrees?
Thou know'st we work by wit and not by witchcraft,
And wit depends on dilatory[125] time.
360   Does't not go well? Cassio hath beaten thee,
And thou by that small hurt hast cashier'd[126] Cassio
Though other things grow fair against the sun,
Yet fruits that blossom first will first be ripe:
Content thyself awhile. By the mass, 'tis morning;
365   Pleasure and action make the hours seem short.
Retire thee; go where thou art billeted:[127]
Away, I say. Thou shalt know more hereafter:
Nay, get thee gone.   *Exit Roderigo.*
Two things are to be done:
370   My wife must move[128] for Cassio to her mistress;
I'll set her on;
Myself the while to draw the Moor apart,
And bring him jump[129] when he may Cassio find
Soliciting his wife: Ay, that's the way;
375   Dull not device by coldness and delay.

                                             Exeunt.

125slow-moving

126discharged

127housed

128plead

129exactly

ACT III

SCENE I
[Before the castle.]

Enter Cassio, with Musicians, and the Clown.

CASSIO: Masters, play here, I will content your pains; Something
    that's brief; and bid "Good morrow, general."[1]

                                                 [1] *i.e., something that will pleasantly awaken the general*

CLOWN: Why, masters, have your instruments been in Naples,
    that they speak i' the nose thus?

5 FIRST MUSICIAN: How, sir, how?

CLOWN: Are these, I pray you, wind instruments?

FIRST MUSICIAN: Ay, marry, are they, sir.

CLOWN: O, thereby hangs a tail.

FIRST MUSICIAN: Whereby hangs a tale, sir?

10 CLOWN: Marry, sir. But, masters, here's money for you; and
    the general so likes your music, that he desires you, for
    love's sake, to make no more noise with it.

FIRST MUSICIAN. Well, sir, we will not.

CLOWN: If you have any music that may not be heard, to't

15   again; but, as they say, to hear music the general does not
    greatly care.

FIRST MUSICIAN: We have none such, sir.

CLOWN: Then put up your pipes in your bag, for I'll away. Go,
    vanish into air, away!   *[Exeunt Musicians.]*

20 CASSIO: Dost thou hear, my honest friend?

CLOWN: No, I hear not your honest friend; I hear you.

CASSIO: Prithee, keep up thy quillets.[2] There's a poor piece of
    gold for thee. If the gentlewoman that attends the general's
    wife be stirring, tell her there's one Cassio entreats her a

                                                 [2] *wisecracks*

25   little favor of speech. Wilt thou do this?

CLOWN: She is stirring, sir. If she will stir hither, I shall seem
    to notify unto her.

CASSIO: Do, good my friend.   [Exit Clown.]

[Enter Iago.]
   In happy time, Iago.
30   IAGO: You have not been abed, then?
   CASSIO: Why, no; the day had broke
       Before we parted. I have made bold, Iago,
       To send in to your wife. My suit to her
       Is that she will to virtuous Desdemona
35   Procure me some access.
   IAGO: I'll send her to you presently;
       And I'll devise a mean³ to draw the Moor
       Out of the way, that your converse and business
       May be more free.
40   CASSIO: I humbly thank you for't. Exit [Iago.] I never knew
       A Florentine more kind and honest.

   Enter Emilia.

   EMILIA: Good morrow, good lieutenant. I am sorry
       For your displeasure, but all will sure be well.
       The general and his wife are talking of it,
45   And she speaks for you stoutly. The Moor replies
       That he you hurt is of great fame in Cyprus
       And great affinity, and that in wholesome wisdom
       He might not but refuse you; but he protests he loves you,
       And needs no other suitor⁴ but his likings
50   To take the safest occasion by the front
       To bring you in again.
   CASSIO: Yet, I beseech you,
       If you think fit, or that it may be done,
       Give me advantage of some brief discourse
55   With Desdemona alone.
   EMILIA: Pray you, come in.
       I will bestow you where you shall have time
       To speak your bosom freely.
   CASSIO: I am much bound to you.
                                        Exeunt.

³means

⁴persuasion

[SCENE II]
[A room in the castle.]

Enter Othello, Iago, and other Gentlemen.

OTHELLO: These letters give, Iago, to the pilot;
  And by him do my duties to the Senate:
  That done, I will be walking on the works;[5]
  Repair there to me.

5 IAGO: Well, my good lord, I'll do't.
OTHELLO: This fortification, gentlemen, shall we see't?
GENTLEMEN: We'll wait upon your lordship.

                    Exeunt.

[5]*defensive structures*

[SCENE III]
[The garden of the castle.]

Enter Desdemona, Cassio, and Emilia.

DESD: Be thou assured, good Cassio, I will do
  All my abilities in thy behalf.
EMILIA: Good madam, do: I warrant it grieves my husband
  As if the cause were his.
5 DESD: O, that's an honest fellow. Do not doubt, Cassio,
  But I will have my lord and you again
  As friendly as you were.
CASSIO: Bounteous madam,
  Whatever shall become of Michael Cassio,
10   He's never anything but your true servant.
DESD: I know't: I thank you. You do love my lord;
  You have known him long; and be you well assured
  He shall in strangeness stand no farther off
  Than in a politic[6] distance.
15 CASSIO: Ay, but, lady,
  That policy[7] may either last so long,
  Or feed upon such nice and waterish[8] diet,
  Or breed itself so out of circumstances,
  That I being absent and my place supplied,
20   My general will forget my love and service.

[6]*appropriate*

[7]*Othello's anger*

[8]*insubstantial*

DESD: Do not doubt that. Before Emilia here
    I give thee warrant of thy place, assure thee,
    If I do vow a friendship, I'll perform it
    To the last article. My lord shall never rest;
25   I'll watch him tame and talk him out of patience;
    His bed shall seem a school, his board a shrift;[9]
    I'll intermingle everything he does
    With Cassio's suit. Therefore be merry, Cassio,
    For thy solicitor[10] shall rather die
30   Than give thy cause away.

Enter Othello, and Iago, at a distance.

EMILIA: Madam, here comes my lord.
CASSIO: Madam, I'll take my leave.
DESD: Nay, stay and hear me speak.
CASSIO: Madam, not now. I am very ill at ease,
35   Unfit for mine own purposes.
DESD: Well, do your discretion.[11]   *Exit [Cassio.]*

Enter Othello and Iago.

IAGO: Ha! I like not that.
OTHELLO: What dost thou say?
IAGO: Nothing, my lord; or if I know not what.
40 OTHELLO: Was not that Cassio parted from my wife?
IAGO: Cassio, my lord! No, sure, I cannot think it,
    That he would steal away so guiltylike,
    Seeing you coming.
OTHELLO: I do believe 'twas he.
45 DESD: How now, my lord!
    I have been talking with a suitor here,
    A man that languishes[12] in your displeasure.
OTHELLO: Who is't you mean?
DESD: Why, your lieutenant, Cassio. Good my lord,
50   If I have any grace or power to move you,
    His present reconciliation take;
    For if he be not one that truly loves you,
    That errs in ignorance and not in cunning,
    I have no judgement in an honest face:
55   I prithee, call him back.

[9] *confession stall; to shrive is to grant forgiveness.*

[10] *person pleading on your behalf*

[11] *judgment*

[12] *wastes away*

OTHELLO: Went he hence now?

DESD: Ay, sooth;[13] so humbled,

    That he hath left part of his grief with me,

    To suffer with him. Good love, call him back.

60 OTHELLO: Not now, sweet Desdemona; some other time.

DESD: But shall't be shortly?

OTHELLO: The sooner, sweet, for you.

DESD: Shall't be tonight at supper?

OTHELLO: No, not tonight.

65 DESD: Tomorrow dinner then?

OTHELLO: I shall not dine at home;

    I meet the captains at the citadel.

DESD: Why then tomorrow night, or Tuesday morn;

    On Tuesday noon, or night, on Wednesday morn;

70   I prithee, name the time, but let it not

    Exceed three days. In faith, he's penitent;

    And yet his trespass,[14] in our common reason—

    Save that, they say, the wars must make examples

    Out of their best—is not almost[15] a fault

75   To incur a private check. When shall he come?

    Tell me, Othello. I wonder in my soul,

    What you would ask me, that I should deny,

    Or stand so mammering[16] on. What? Michael Cassio,

    That came awooing with you, and so many a time

80   When I have spoke of you dispraisingly

    Hath ta'en your part—to have so much to do

    To bring him in! Trust me, I could do much—

OTHELLO: Prithee, no more. Let him come when he will;

    I will deny thee nothing.

85 DESD: Why, this is not a boon;

    'Tis as I should entreat you wear your gloves,

    Or feed on nourishing dishes, or keep you warm,

    Or sue to you to do a peculiar profit

    To your own person. Nay, when I have a suit—

90   Wherein I mean to touch your love indeed,

    It shall be full of poise and difficult weight,

    And fearful to be granted.

OTHELLO: I will deny thee nothing:

    Whereon, I do beseech thee, grant me this,

95   To leave me but a little to myself.

DESD: Shall I deny you? No. Farewell, my lord.

[13] *in truth*

[14] *mistake*

[15] *hardly*

[16] *delaying*

OTHELLO: Farewell, my Desdemona; I'll come to thee straight.

DESD: Emilia, come. Be as your fancies teach you; Whate'er
you be, I am obedient. *[Exeunt Desdemona and Emilia.]*

100 OTHELLO: Excellent wretch! Perdition catch my soul,
But I do love thee! and when I love thee not,
Chaos is come again.

IAGO: My noble lord—

OTHELLO: What dost thou say, Iago?

105 IAGO: Did Michael Cassio, when you woo'd my lady,
Know of your love?

OTHELLO: He did, from first to last. Why dost thou ask?

IAGO: But for a satisfaction of my thought;
No further harm.

110 OTHELLO: Why of thy thought, Iago?

IAGO: I did not think he had been acquainted with her.

OTHELLO: O, yes, and went between us very oft.

IAGO: Indeed!

OTHELLO: Indeed? ay, indeed. Discern'st thou aught in that?

115   Is he not honest?

IAGO: Honest, my lord?

OTHELLO: Honest? Ay, honest.

IAGO: My lord, for aught I know.

OTHELLO: What dost thou think?

120 IAGO: Think, my lord?

OTHELLO: Think, my lord? By heaven, he echoes me,
As if there were some monster in his thought
Too hideous to be shown. Thou dost mean something:
I heard thee say even now, thou like'st not that,

125   When Cassio left my wife. What didst not like?
And when I told thee he was of my counsel
In my whole course of wooing, thou criedst, "Indeed!"
And didst contract and purse[17] thy brow together,
As if thou then hadst shut up in thy brain

130   Some horrible conceit. If thou dost love me,
Show me thy thought.

IAGO: My lord, you know I love you.

OTHELLO: I think thou dost;
And for I know thou'rt full of love and honesty

135   And weigh'st thy words before thou givest them breath,
Therefore these stops of thine fright me the more;

[17]*wrinkle; draw
together*

For such things in a false disloyal knave
Are tricks of custom; but in a man that's just
They're close dilations,[18] working from the heart,

140   That passion cannot rule.[19]

IAGO: For Michael Cassio,
I dare be sworn I think that he is honest.

OTHELLO: I think so too.

IAGO: Men should be what they seem;

145   Or those that be not, would they might seem none!

OTHELLO: Certain, men should be what they seem.

IAGO: Why then I think Cassio's an honest man.

OTHELLO: Nay, yet there's more in this:
I prithee, speak to me as to thy thinkings,

150   As thou dost ruminate, and give thy worst of thoughts
The worst of words.

IAGO: Good my lord, pardon me;
Though I am bound to every act of duty,
I am not bound to that all slaves are free to.[20]

155   Utter my thoughts? Why, say they are vile and false;
As where's that palace whereinto foul things
Sometimes intrude not? Who has a breast so pure,
But some uncleanly apprehensions[21]
Keep leets and lawdays,[22] and in session sit

160   With meditations lawful?

OTHELLO: Thou dost conspire against thy friend, Iago,
If thou but think'st him wrong'd and makest his ear
A stranger to thy thoughts.

IAGO: I do beseech you—

165   Though I perchance am vicious in my guess,
As, I confess, it is my nature's plague
To spy into abuses, and oft my jealousy
Shapes faults that are not—that your wisdom yet,
From one that so imperfectly conceits,[23]

170   Would take no notice, nor build yourself a trouble
Out of his scattering and unsure observance.
It were not for your quiet nor your good,
Nor for my manhood, honesty, or wisdom,
To let you know my thoughts.

175 OTHELLO: What dost thou mean?

IAGO: Good name in man and woman, dear my lord,

[18]*accusations*

[19]*i.e., that cannot be kept back*

[20]*the duty to reveal my thoughts*

[21]*suspicions*

[22]*hold court*

[23]*gets ideas*

Is the immediate jewel of their souls:
Who steals my purse steals trash; 'tis something, nothing;
'Twas mine, 'tis his, and has been slave to thousands;
180   But he that filches from me my good name
Robs me of that which not enriches him
And makes me poor indeed.
OTHELLO: By heaven, I'll know thy thoughts.
IAGO: You cannot, if my heart were in your hand;
185   Nor shall not, whilst 'tis in my custody.
OTHELLO: Ha!
IAGO: O, beware, my lord, of jealousy!
It is the green-eyed monster, which doth mock
The meat it feeds on. That cuckold[24] lives in bliss
190   Who, certain of his fate, loves not his wronger;
But O, what damned minutes tells[25] he o'er
Who dotes, yet doubts, suspects, yet strongly loves!
OTHELLO: O misery!
IAGO: Poor and content is rich, and rich enough;
195   But riches fineless[26] is as poor as winter
To him that ever fears he shall be poor.
Good heaven, the souls of all my tribe defend
From jealousy!
OTHELLO: Why, why is this?
200   Think'st thou I'ld make a life of jealousy,
To follow still the changes of the moon
With fresh suspicions?[27] No! To be once in doubt
Is once to be resolved. Exchange me for a goat,
When I shall turn the business of my soul
205   To such exsufflicate and blown surmises,[28]
Matching thy inference. 'Tis not to make me jealous
To say my wife is fair, feeds well, loves company,
Is free of speech, sings, plays, and dances well;
Where virtue is, these are more virtuous.
210   Nor from mine own weak merits will I draw
The smallest fear or doubt of her revolt;
For she had eyes and chose me.
No, Iago, I'll see before I doubt; when I doubt, prove;
And on the proof, there is no more but this,
215   Away at once with love or jealousy!
IAGO: I am glad of it, for now I shall have reason

[24]*man whose wife cheats on him*

[25]*counts*

[26]*without bounds*

[27]*i.e., change suspicions as often as the moon changes*

[28]*inflated and overblown guesses*

To show the love and duty that I bear you
With franker spirit. Therefore, as I am bound,
Receive it from me. I speak not yet of proof.
220   Look to your wife; observe her well with Cassio;
Wear your eye thus, not jealous nor secure.
I would not have your free and noble nature
Out of selfbounty[29] be abused. Look to't.
I know our country disposition well;
225   In Venice they do let heaven see the pranks
They dare not show their husbands; their best conscience
Is not to leave't undone, but keep't unknown.

OTHELLO: Dost thou say so?

IAGO: She did deceive her father, marrying you;
230   And when she seem'd to shake and fear your looks,
She loved them most.

OTHELLO: And so she did.

IAGO: Why, go to then.
She that so young could give out such a seeming,
235   To seel her father's eyes up close as oak—
He thought 'twas witchcraft—but I am much to blame;
I humbly do beseech you of your pardon
For too much loving you.

OTHELLO: I am bound to thee forever.
240 IAGO: I see this hath a little dash'd your spirits.

OTHELLO: Not a jot, not a jot.

IAGO: I' faith, I fear it has.
I hope you will consider what is spoke
Comes from my love. But I do see you're moved;
245   I am to pray you not to strain my speech
To grosser[30] issues, nor to larger reach
Than to suspicion.

OTHELLO: I will not.

IAGO: Should you do so, my lord,
250   My speech should fall into such vile success
Which my thoughts aim not at. Cassio's my worthy friend—
My lord, I see you're moved.

OTHELLO: No, not much moved.
I do not think but Desdemona's honest.
255 IAGO: Long live she so! and long live you to think so!

OTHELLO: And yet, how nature erring from itself—

[29]*generosity of spirit*

[30]*baser, more rude*

IAGO: Ay, there's the point, as—to be bold with you—
    Not to affect[31] many proposed matches
    Of her own clime, complexion, and degree,
260   Whereto we see in all things nature tends—
    Foh, one may smell in such a will most rank,
    Foul disproportion, thoughts unnatural.
    But pardon me. I do not in position[32]
    Distinctly speak of her; though I may fear,
265   Her will, recoiling to her better judgement,
    May fall[33] to match you with her country forms,
    And happily repent.
OTHELLO: Farewell, farewell:
    If more thou dost perceive, let me know more;
270   Set on thy wife to observe. Leave me, Iago.
IAGO: My lord, I take my leave.
OTHELLO: Why did I marry? This honest creature doubtless
    Sees and knows more, much more, than he unfolds.
IAGO: My lord, I would I might entreat your honor
275   To scan this thing no further; leave it to time:
    Though it be fit that Cassio have his place,
    For sure he fills it up with great ability,
    Yet, if you please to hold him off awhile,
    You shall by that perceive him and his means:
280   Note if your lady strain[34] his entertainment[35]
    With any strong or vehement importunity;
    Much will be seen in that. In the meantime,
    Let me be thought too busy in my fears—
    As worthy cause I have to fear I am—
285   And hold her free, I do beseech your honor.
OTHELLO: Fear not my government.
IAGO: I once more take my leave.   *Exit.*
OTHELLO: This fellow's of exceeding honesty,
    And knows all qualities, with a learned spirit,
290   Of human dealings. If I do prove her haggard,[36]
    Though that her jesses[37] were my dear heartstrings,
    I'd whistle her off[38] and let her down the wind
    To prey at fortune.[39] Haply, for I am black
    And have not those soft parts of conversation
295   That chamberers[40] have, or for I am declined
    Into the vale of years—yet that's not much—

[31] *find attractive*

[32] *my assertion*

[33] *happen*

[34] *insist*

[35] *that you entertain, or listen to, him*

[36] *unprincipled; in the next lines, Othello compares Desdemona to a bird used in falconry.*

[37] *leashes*

[38] *let her go*

[39] *as she wished*

[40] *gentlemen*

　　　　She's gone. I am abused, and my relief
　　　　Must be to loathe her. O curse of marriage,
　　　　That we can call these delicate creatures ours,
300　　And not their appetites! I had rather be a toad,
　　　　And live upon the vapor of a dungeon,
　　　　Than keep a corner in the thing I love
　　　　For others' uses. Yet, 'tis the plague of great ones;
　　　　Prerogatived[41] are they less than the base;
305　　'Tis destiny unshunnable, like death:
　　　　Even then this forked plague[42] is fated to us
　　　　When we do quicken. Desdemona comes:

Enter Desdemona and Emilia.
　　　　If she be false, O, then heaven mocks itself!
　　　　I'll not believe't.
310　DESD:　How now, my dear Othello!
　　　　Your dinner, and the generous islanders
　　　　By you invited, do attend your presence.
　　OTHELLO: I am to blame.
　　DESD:　Why do you speak so faintly?
315　　Are you not well?
　　OTHELLO: I have a pain upon my forehead here.
　　DESD:　Faith, that's with watching; 'twill away again:
　　　　Let me but bind it hard, within this hour
　　　　It will be well.
320　OTHELLO: Your napkin is too little;
　　　　　　[He puts the handkerchief from him, and she drops it.]
　　　　Let it alone. Come, I'll go in with you.
　　DESD: I am very sorry that you are not well.
　　　　　　　　　　　　　Exeunt Othello and Desdemona.
　　EMILIA: I am glad I have found this napkin:
　　　　This was her first remembrance[43] from the Moor:
325　　My wayward husband hath a hundred times
　　　　Woo'd[44] me to steal it; but she so loves the token,
　　　　For he conjured her she should ever keep it,
　　　　That she reserves it evermore about her
　　　　To kiss and talk to. I'll have the work ta'en out,
330　　And give't Iago. What he will do with it
　　　　Heaven knows, not I;
　　　　I nothing but to please his fantasy.

[41]*privileged*

[42]*the curse of having a cuckold's horns [Men who were the victims of adultery were commonly pictured with horns.]*

[43]*gift*

[44]*coaxed*

Enter Iago.

IAGO: How now, what do you here alone?
EMILIA: Do not you chide; I have a thing for you.
335 IAGO: A thing for me? It is a common thing—
EMILIA: Ha!
IAGO: To have a foolish wife.
EMILIA: O, is that all? What will you give me now
    For that same handkerchief?
340 IAGO: What handkerchief?
EMILIA: What handkerchief?
    Why, that the Moor first gave to Desdemona;
    That which so often you did bid me steal.
IAGO: Hast stol'n it from her?
345 EMILIA: No, faith; she let it drop by negligence,
    And, to the advantage, I being here took't up.
    Look, here it is.
IAGO: A good wench; give it me.
EMILIA: What will you do with't, that you have been so
350   earnest
    To have me filch it?
IAGO: Why, what is that to you?
EMILIA: If't be not for some purpose of import,
    Give't me again. Poor lady, she'll run mad
355   When she shall lack it.
IAGO: Be not acknown on't;[45] I have use for it.
    Go, leave me.   *Exit Emilia.*
    I will in Cassio's lodging lose this napkin,
    And let him find it. Trifles light as air
360   Are to the jealous confirmations strong
    As proofs of holy writ;[46] this may do something.
    The Moor already changes with my poison:
    Dangerous conceits are in their natures poisons,
    Which at the first are scarce found to distaste,
365   But with a little act upon the blood
    Burn like the mines of sulphur. I did say so:
    Look, where he comes!

Enter Othello.
    Not poppy, nor mandragora,[47]
    Nor all the drowsy syrups of the world,

[45] *do not admit you know about it*

[46] *Scripture*

[47] *sleep-inducing plants*

370   Shall ever medicine thee to that sweet sleep
        Which thou owedst yesterday.
    OTHELLO: Ha, ha, false to me?
    IAGO: Why, how now, general! No more of that.
    OTHELLO: Avaunt! be gone! Thou hast set me on the rack:
375   I swear 'tis better to be much abused
        Than but to know't a little.
    IAGO: How now, my lord?
    OTHELLO: What sense had I of her stol'n hours of lust?
        I saw't not, thought it not, it harm'd not me;
380   I slept the next night well, was free and merry;
        I found not Cassio's kisses on her lips:
        He that is robb'd, not wanting what is stol'n,
        Let him not know't and he's not robb'd at all.
    IAGO: I am sorry to hear this.
385 OTHELLO: I had been happy if the general camp,
        Pioners[48] and all, had tasted her sweet body,
        So I had nothing known. O, now forever
        Farewell the tranquil mind! Farewell content!
        Farewell the plumed troop and the big wars
390   That make ambition virtue! O, farewell,
        Farewell the neighing steed and the shrill trump,
        The spiritstirring drum, the earpiercing fife,
        The royal banner, and all quality,
        Pride, pomp, and circumstance of glorious war!
395   And O you mortal engines, whose rude throats
        The immortal Jove's dread clamors counterfeit,
        Farewell! Othello's occupation's gone!
    IAGO: Is't possible, my lord?
    OTHELLO: Villain, be sure thou prove my love a whore;
400   Be sure of it. Give me the ocular[49] proof;
        Or, by the worth of man's eternal soul,
        Thou hadst been better have been born a dog
        Than answer my waked wrath!
    IAGO: Is't come to this?
405 OTHELLO: Make me to see't; or at the least so prove it,
        That the probation bear no hinge nor loop
        To hang a doubt on; or woe upon thy life!
    IAGO: My noble lord
    OTHELLO: If thou dost slander her and torture me,
410   Never pray more; abandon all remorse;

[48]*laborers*

[49]*visible*

On horror's head horrors accumulate.
Do deeds to make heaven weep, all earth amazed;
For nothing canst thou to damnation add
Greater than that.

415 IAGO: O grace! O heaven defend me!
Are you a man? have you a soul or sense?
God be wi' you; take mine office. O wretched fool,
That livest to make thine honesty a vice!
O monstrous world! Take note, take note, O world,
420 To be direct and honest is not safe.
I thank you for this profit, and from hence
I'll love no friend sith love breeds such offense.

OTHELLO: Nay, stay; thou shouldst be honest.

IAGO: I should be wise; for honesty's a fool,
425 And loses that it works for.

OTHELLO: By the world,
I think my wife be honest, and think she is not;
I think that thou art just, and think thou art not.
I'll have some proof. Her name, that was as fresh
430 As Dian's visage, is now begrimed and black
As mine own face. If there be cords or knives,
Poison or fire, or suffocating streams,
I'll not endure it. Would I were satisfied!

IAGO: I see, sir, you are eaten up with passion;
435 I do repent me that I put it to you.
You would be satisfied?

OTHELLO: Would? Nay, I will.

IAGO: And may. But, how? how satisfied, my lord?
Would you, the supervisor, grossly gape on?
440 Behold her topp'd?

OTHELLO: Death and damnation! O!

IAGO: It were a tedious difficulty, I think,
To bring them to that prospect. Damn them then,
If ever mortal eyes do see them bolster
445 More than their own![50] What then? how then?
What shall I say? Where's satisfaction?
It is impossible you should see this
Were they as prime[51] as goats, as hot as monkeys,
As salt[52] as wolves in pride, and fools as gross
450 As ignorance made drunk. But yet, I say,
If imputation and strong circumstances,

[50]*their own eyes (i.e., No one besides themselves will ever catch them.)*

[51]*lustful*

[52]*lecherous*

Which lead directly to the door of truth,
Will give you satisfaction, you may have't.
OTHELLO: Give me a living reason she's disloyal.
455 IAGO: I do not like the office;
But sith I am enter'd in this cause so far,
Prick'd to't by foolish honesty and love,
I will go on. I lay with Cassio lately
And, being troubled with a raging tooth,
460 I could not sleep.
There are a kind of men so loose of soul,
That in their sleeps will mutter their affairs;
One of this kind is Cassio
In sleep I heard him say, "Sweet Desdemona,
465 Let us be wary, let us hide our loves";
And then, sir, would he gripe and wring my hand,
Cry, "O sweet creature!" and then kiss me hard,
As if he pluck'd up kisses by the roots,
That grew upon my lips; then laid his leg
470 Over my thigh, and sigh'd and kiss'd; and then
Cried, "Cursed fate that gave thee to the Moor!"
OTHELLO: O monstrous! monstrous!
IAGO: Nay, this was but his dream.
OTHELLO: But this denoted a foregone conclusion:
475 'Tis a shrewd doubt, though it be but a dream.
IAGO: And this may help to thicken other proofs
That do demonstrate thinly.
OTHELLO: I'll tear her all to pieces.
IAGO: Nay, but be wise; yet we see nothing done;
480 She may be honest yet. Tell me but this;
Have you not sometimes seen a handkerchief
Spotted with strawberries in your wife's hand?
OTHELLO: I gave her such a one; 'twas my first gift.
IAGO: I know not that; but such a handkerchief—
485 I am sure it was your wife's—did I today
See Cassio wipe his beard with.
OTHELLO: If it be that—
IAGO: If it be that, or any that was hers,
It speaks against her with the other proofs.
490 OTHELLO: O, that the slave had forty thousand lives!
One is too poor, too weak for my revenge.
Now do I see 'tis true. Look here, Iago;

All my fond love thus do I blow to heaven:

'Tis gone.

495   Arise, black vengeance, from thy hollow cell!

Yield up, O love, thy crown and hearted throne

To tyrannous hate! Swell, bosom, with thy fraught,[53]

For 'tis of aspics' tongues!

IAGO: Yet be content.

500   OTHELLO: O, blood, blood, blood!

IAGO: Patience, I say; your mind perhaps may change.

OTHELLO: Never, Iago: Like to the Pontic Sea,[54]

Whose icy current and compulsive course

Ne'er feels retiring[55] ebb, but keeps due on

505   To the Propontic and the Hellespont,

Even so my bloody thoughts, with violent pace,

Shall ne'er look back, ne'er ebb to humble love,

Till that a capable and wide revenge

Swallow them up. Now, by yond marble heaven,

510   In the due reverence of a sacred vow

I here engage my words.

IAGO: Do not rise yet.

Witness, you everburning lights above,

You elements that clip us round about,   *Iago Kneels.*

515   Witness that here Iago doth give up

The execution of his wit, hands, heart,

To wrong'd Othello's service! Let him command,

And to obey shall be in me remorse,

What bloody business ever.

520   OTHELLO: I greet thy love,

Not with vain thanks, but with acceptance bounteous,

And will upon the instant put thee to't:

Within these three days let me hear thee say

That Cassio's not alive.

525   IAGO: My friend is dead, 'tis done at your request;

But let her live.

OTHELLO: Damn her, lewd minx! O, damn her!

Come, go with me apart; I will withdraw,

To furnish me with some swift means of death

530   For the fair devil. Now art thou my lieutenant.

IAGO: I am your own forever.   *Exeunt.*

---

[53]*load*

[54]*the Black Sea, which always seems to move forward*

[55]*retreating*

[SCENE IV]
[Before the castle.]

Enter Desdemona, Emilia, and Clown.

DESD: Do you know, sirrah, where Lieutenant Cassio lies?

CLOWN. I dare not say he lies anywhere.

DESD: Why, man?

CLOWN. He's a soldier; and for one to say a soldier lies, is stab-
5   bing.

DESD: Go to! Where lodges he?

CLOWN. To tell you where he lodges, is to tell you where I lie.

DESD: Can anything be made of this?

CLOWN. I know not where he lodges, and for me to devise a
10   lodging, and say he lies here or he lies there, were to lie in
    mine own throat.

DESD: Can you inquire him out and be edified[56] by report?   [56]*instructed*

CLOWN. I will catechize the world for him; that is, make ques-
    tions and by them answer.

15 DESD: Seek him, bid him come hither. Tell him I have moved
    my lord on his behalf and hope all will be well.

CLOWN. To do this is within the compass of man's wit, and
    therefore I will attempt the doing it.   *[Exit.]*

DESD: Where should I lose that handkerchief, Emilia?

20 EMILIA: I know not, madam.

DESD: Believe me, I had rather have lost my purse
    Full of crusadoes;[57] and, but my noble Moor   [57]*gold coins*
    Is true of mind and made of no such baseness
    As jealous creatures are, it were enough
25   To put him to ill thinking.

EMILIA: Is he not jealous?

DESD: Who, he? I think the sun where he was born
    Drew all such humors from him.

EMILIA: Look, where he comes.

30 DESD: I will not leave him now till Cassio
    Be call'd to him.

Enter Othello.

    How is't with you, my lord?

[58] disguise (my anger)

OTHELLO: Well, my good lady. O, hardness to dissemble![58]
How do you, Desdemona?

35 DESD: Well, my good lord.

OTHELLO: Give me your hand. This hand is moist, my lady.

DESD: It yet has felt no age nor known no sorrow:

OTHELLO: This argues fruitfulness and liberal heart;
Hot, hot, and moist. This hand of yours requires

[59] withdrawal

40 A sequester[59] from liberty, fasting and prayer,

[60] purification

Much castigation,[60] exercise devout,
For here's a young and sweating devil here
That commonly rebels. 'Tis a good hand,
A frank one.

45 DESD: You may, indeed, say so;
For 'twas that hand that gave away my heart.

OTHELLO: A liberal hand. The hearts of old gave hands;
But our new heraldry is hands, not hearts.[61]

[61] i.e., People's hearts once gave away their hands in marriage; now their hands offer up their hearts too easily.

DESD: I cannot speak of this. Come now, your promise.

50 OTHELLO: What promise, chuck?[62]

DESD: I have sent to bid Cassio come speak with you.

[62] a term of affection (but less flattering than the terms Othello used earlier)

OTHELLO: I have a salt and sorry rheum[63] offends me;
Lend me thy handkerchief.

DESD: Here, my lord.

[63] cold

55 OTHELLO: That which I gave you.

DESD: I have it not about me.

OTHELLO: Not?

DESD: No, faith, my lord.

OTHELLO: That's a fault. That handkerchief
60 Did an Egyptian to my mother give;
She was a charmer, and could almost read
The thoughts of people. She told her, while she kept it,
'Twould make her amiable and subdue my father
Entirely to her love, but if she lost it
65 Or made a gift of it, my father's eye
Should hold her loathed and his spirits should hunt
After new fancies. She dying gave it me,
And bid me, when my fate would have me wive,
To give it her. I did so, and take heed on't;
70 Make it a darling like your precious eye;
To lose't or give't away were such perdition[64]
As nothing else could match.

[64] ruin

DESD: Is't possible?

OTHELLO: 'Tis true; there's magic in the web of it.

75　　A sibyl,[65] that had number'd in the world

　　　The sun to course two hundred compasses,

　　　In her prophetic fury sew'd the work;

　　　The worms were hallow'd that did breed the silk,

　　　And it was dyed in mummy which the skillful

80　　Conserved of maidens' hearts.

DESD: Indeed! is't true?

OTHELLO: Most veritable; therefore look to't well.

DESD: Then would to God that I had never seen't!

OTHELLO: Ha! wherefore?

85　DESD: Why do you speak so startingly and rash?

OTHELLO: Is't lost? is't gone? speak, is it out o' the way?

DESD: Heaven bless us!

OTHELLO: Say you?

DESD: It is not lost; but what an if it were?

90　OTHELLO: How?

DESD: I say, it is not lost.

OTHELLO: Fetch't, let me see it.

DESD: Why, so I can, sir, but I will not now.

　　　This is a trick to put me from my suit.

95　　Pray you, let Cassio be received again.

OTHELLO: Fetch me the handkerchief, my mind misgives.

DESD: Come, come; You'll never meet a more sufficient man.

OTHELLO: The handkerchief!

DESD: I pray, talk me of Cassio:

100　OTHELLO: The handkerchief!

DESD: A man that all his time

　　　Hath founded his good fortunes on your love,

　　　Shared dangers with you—

OTHELLO: The handkerchief!

105　DESD: In sooth, you are to blame.

OTHELLO: Away!　　　　　　　　　　　　　　　*Exit.*

EMILIA: Is not this man jealous?

DESD: I ne'er saw this before.

　　　Sure there's some wonder in this handkerchief;

110　　I am most unhappy in the loss of it.

EMILIA: 'Tis not a year or two shows us a man:

　　　They are all but stomachs and we all but food;

[65]*prophetess, fortune-teller*

They eat us hungerly, and when they are full
They belch us. Look you! Cassio and my husband.

Enter Iago and Cassio.

115 IAGO: There is no other way; 'tis she must do't:
 And, lo, the happiness! Go and importune her.
DESD: How now, good Cassio! What's the news with you?
CASSIO: Madam, my former suit: I do beseech you
 That by your virtuous means I may again
120 Exist and be a member of his love
 Whom I with all the office of my heart
 Entirely honor. I would not be delay'd.
 If my offense be of such mortal kind
 That nor my service past nor present sorrows
125 Nor purposed[66] merit in futurity
 Can ransom me into his love again,
 But to know so must be my benefit;
 So shall I clothe me in a forced content
 And shut myself up in some other course
130 To Fortune's alms.
DESD: Alas, thrice gentle Cassio!
 My advocation is not now in tune;
 My lord is not my lord, nor should I know him
 Were he in favor as in humor alter'd.
135 So help me every spirit sanctified,
 As I have spoken for you all my best
 And stood within the blank of his displeasure
 For my free speech! You must awhile be patient.
 What I can do I will; and more I will
140 Than for myself I dare. Let that suffice you.
IAGO: Is my lord angry?
EMILIA: He went hence but now,
 And certainly in strange unquietness.
IAGO: Can he be angry? I have seen the cannon,
145 When it hath blown his ranks into the air
 And, like the devil, from his very arm
 Puff'd his own brother. And can he be angry?
 Something of moment then. I will go meet him:
 There's matter in't indeed if he be angry.
150 DESD: I prithee, do so.   *Exit Iago.*

[66] *intentional*

Something sure of state,[67]
Either from Venice or some unhatch'd practice
Made demonstrable here in Cyprus to him,
Hath puddled his clear spirit; and in such cases
155 Men's natures wrangle with inferior things,
Though great ones are their object. 'Tis even so;
For let our finger ache, and it indues[68]
Our other healthful members even to that sense
Of pain. Nay, we must think men are not gods,
160 Nor of them look for such observancy
As fits the bridal. Beshrew me much, Emilia,
I was, unhandsome warrior as I am,
Arraigning[69] his unkindness with my soul;
But now I find I had suborn'd[70] the witness,
165 And he's indicted falsely.
EMILIA: Pray heaven it be state matters, as you think,
And no conception nor no jealous toy[71]
Concerning you.
DESD: Alas the day, I never gave him cause!
170 EMILIA: But jealous souls will not be answer'd so;
They are not ever jealous for the cause,
But jealous for they are jealous. 'Tis a monster
Begot upon itself, born on itself.
DESD: Heaven keep that monster from Othello's mind!
175 EMILIA: Lady, amen.
DESD: I will go seek him. Cassio, walk hereabout.
If I do find him fit, I'll move your suit,
And seek to effect it to my uttermost.
CASSIO: I humbly thank your ladyship.

> *Exeunt Desdemona and Emilia.*

Enter Bianca.

180 BIANCA: Save you, friend Cassio!
CASSIO: What make you from home?
How is it with you, my most fair Bianca?
I'faith, sweet love, I was coming to your house.
BIANCA: And I was going to your lodging, Cassio
185 What, keep a week away? seven days and nights?
Eight score eight hours? and lovers' absent hours,
More tedious than the dial eight score times?
O weary reckoning!

[67] *official business*

[68] *leads*

[69] *putting on trial*

[70] *committed perjury against*

[71] *notion*

⁷²*undisturbed*

CASSIO: Pardon me, Bianca:
190   I have this while with leaden thoughts been press'd;
    But I shall in a more continuate[72] time
    Strike off this score of absence. Sweet Bianca,
    Take me this work out.
BIANCA: O Cassio, whence came this?
195   This is some token from a newer friend.
    To the felt absence now I feel a cause:
    Is't come to this? Well, well.
CASSIO: Go to, woman!
    Throw your vile guesses in the devil's teeth,
200   From whence you have them. You are jealous now
    That this is from some mistress, some remembrance:
    No, by my faith, Bianca.
BIANCA: Why, whose is it?
CASSIO: I know not, sweet. I found it in my chamber.
205   I like the work well. Ere it be demanded—
    As like enough it will—I'd have it copied:
    Take it, and do't; and leave me for this time.
BIANCA: Leave you! wherefore?

⁷³*advantage*

CASSIO: I do attend here on the general;
210   And think it no addition,[73] nor my wish,
    To have him see me woman'd.
BIANCA: Why, I pray you?
CASSIO: Not that I love you not.
BIANCA: But that you do not love me.
215   I pray you, bring me on the way a little;
    And say if I shall see you soon at night.
CASSIO: 'Tis but a little way that I can bring you;
    For I attend here, but I'll see you soon.

⁷⁴*accept circum-
stances*

BIANCA: 'Tis very good; I must be circumstanced.[74]

Exeunt.

ACT IV

[SCENE I]
[Cyprus. Before the castle.]

Enter Iago and Othello.

IAGO: Will you think so?
OTHELLO: Think so, Iago?
IAGO: What,
    To kiss in private?
5 OTHELLO: An unauthorized kiss.
IAGO: Or to be naked with her friend in bed
    An hour or more, not meaning any harm?
OTHELLO: Naked in bed, Iago, and not mean harm!
    It is hypocrisy against the devil:
10   They that mean virtuously and yet do so,
    The devil their virtue tempts and they tempt heaven.
IAGO: So they do nothing, 'tis a venial[1] slip:
    But if I give my wife a handkerchief
OTHELLO: What then?
15 IAGO: Why, then, 'tis hers, my lord, and being hers,
    She may, I think, bestow't on any man.
OTHELLO: She is protectress of her honor too:
    May she give that?
IAGO: Her honor is an essence that's not seen;
20   They have it very oft that have it not:
    But for the handkerchief—
OTHELLO: By heaven, I would most gladly have forgot it:
    Thou said'st—O, it comes o'er my memory,
    As doth the raven[2] o'er the infected house,
25   Boding to all—he had my handkerchief.
IAGO: Ay, what of that?
OTHELLO: That's not so good now.

[1] *having to do with the flesh; not as serious as mortal matters, which involve the spirit*

[2] *[The raven is thought to bring disease.]*

³*excessive love*

⁴*Iago compares Cassio to scoundrels who, although they have begged for love or received it from infatuated women, brag about having seduced the women.*

⁵*disgusting*

⁶*Nature would not lead me to such anger for no reason.*

IAGO: What if I had said I had seen him do you wrong?
Or heard him say—as knaves be such abroad,
30   Who having, by their own importunate suit,
Or voluntary dotage³ of some mistress,
Convinced or supplied them, cannot choose
But they must blab⁴—
OTHELLO: Hath he said anything?
35 IAGO: He hath, my lord; but be you well assured,
No more than he'll unswear.
OTHELLO: What hath he said?
IAGO: Faith, that he did—I know not what he did.
OTHELLO: What? what?
40 IAGO: Lie—
OTHELLO: With her?
IAGO: With her, on her, what you will.
OTHELLO: Lie with her! lie on her!—We say lie on her, when
they belie her.—Lie with her! 'Zounds, that's fulsome!⁵
45   Handkerchief—confessions—handkerchief! To confess
and be hanged for his labor first, to be hanged, and then
to confess. I tremble at it. Nature would not invest herself
in such shadowing passion without some instruction.⁶ It
is not words that shakes me thus. Pish! Noses, ears, and
50   lips. Is't possible? Confess?—Handkerchief?—O devil!

He falls down [in a trance.]

IAGO: Work on,
My medicine, work! Thus credulous fools are caught:
And many worthy and chaste dames even thus,
All guiltless, meet reproach. What, ho! My lord!
55   My lord, I say! Othello!

Enter Cassio.

How now, Cassio!
CASSIO: What's the matter?
IAGO: My lord is fall'n into an epilepsy:
This is his second fit; he had one yesterday.
60 CASSIO: Rub him about the temples.
IAGO: No, forbear;
The lethargy must have his quiet course:
If not, he foams at mouth, and by and by
Breaks out to savage madness. Look, he stirs:

65 Do you withdraw yourself a little while,
    He will recover straight. When he is gone,
    I would on great occasion speak with you. *[Exit Cassio.]*
    How is it, general? Have you not hurt your head?
OTHELLO: Dost thou mock me?
70 IAGO: I mock you? No, by heaven.
    Would you would bear your fortune like a man!
OTHELLO: A horned man's a monster and a beast.
IAGO: There's many a beast then in a populous city,
    And many a civil monster.
75 OTHELLO: Did he confess it?
IAGO: Good sir, be a man;
    Think every bearded fellow that's but yoked
    May draw with you. There's millions now alive
    That nightly lie in those unproper beds
80 Which they dare swear peculiar.[7] Your case is better.
    O, 'tis the spite of hell, the fiend's archmock,[8]
    To lip a wanton in a secure couch,
    And to suppose her chaste! No, let me know;
    And knowing what I am, I know what she shall be.
85 OTHELLO: O, thou art wise; 'tis certain.
IAGO: Stand you awhile apart;
    Confine yourself but in a patient list.[9]
    Whilst you were here o'erwhelmed with your grief—
    A passion most unsuiting such a man—
90 Cassio came hither. I shifted him away,
    And laid good 'scuse upon your ecstasy;
    Bade him anon return and here speak with me;
    The which he promised. Do but encave yourself,
    And mark the fleers,[10] the gibes,[11] and notable scorns,
95 That dwell in every region of his face;
    For I will make him tell the tale anew,
    Where, how, how oft, how long ago, and when
    He hath and is again to cope[12] your wife:
    I say, but mark his gesture. Marry, patience,
100 Or I shall say you are all in all in spleen,
    And nothing of a man.
OTHELLO: Dost thou hear, Iago?
    I will be found most cunning in my patience;
    But—dost thou hear?—most bloody.

[7]*their own*

[8]*main joke*

[9]*limit*

[10]*mockings*

[11]*jokes*

[12]*join with*

105 IAGO: That's not amiss;
        But yet keep time in all. Will you withdraw?
        Now will I question Cassio of Bianca,
        A housewife that by selling her desires
        Buys herself bread and clothes. It is a creature
110   That dotes on Cassio, as 'tis the strumpet's plague
        To beguile many and be beguiled by one.
        He, when he hears of her, cannot refrain
        From the excess of laughter. Here he comes.

Enter Cassio.
        As he shall smile, Othello shall go mad;

13 *ignorant*

115   And his unbookish[13] jealousy must construe
        Poor Cassio's smiles, gestures, and light behavior,
        Quite in the wrong. How do you now, lieutenant?
  CASSIO: The worser that you give me the addition

14 *the title of "lieu-tenant"*

        Whose want even kills me.[14]
120 IAGO: Ply Desdemona well, and you are sure on't.
        Now, if this suit lay in Bianca's power,
        How quickly should you speed!
  CASSIO: Alas, poor caitiff![15]

15 *wretch*

  OTHELLO: Look, how he laughs already!
125 IAGO: I never knew a woman love man so.
  CASSIO: Alas, poor rogue! I think, i'faith, she loves me.
  OTHELLO: Now he denies it faintly and laughs it out.
  IAGO: Do you hear, Cassio?
  OTHELLO: Now he importunes him
130   To tell it o'er. Go to; well said, well said.
  IAGO: She gives it out that you shall marry her;
        Do you intend it?
  CASSIO: Ha, ha, ha!
  OTHELLO: Do you triumph, Roman? Do you triumph?

16 *credit*

135 CASSIO: I marry her! What? A customer! I prithee, bear some
        charity to my wit;[16] do not think it so unwholesome. Ha,
        ha, ha!
  OTHELLO: So, so, so, so. They laugh that win.
  IAGO: Faith, the cry goes that you shall marry her.
140 CASSIO: Prithee, say true.
  IAGO: I am a very villain else.
  OTHELLO: Have you scored me? Well.

CASSIO: This is the monkey's own giving out. She is persuaded
    I will marry her, out of her own love and flattery, not out
145   of my promise.

OTHELLO: Iago beckons me; now he begins the story.

CASSIO: She was here even now; she haunts me in every place.
    I was the other day talking on the sea bank with certain
    Venetians, and thither comes the bauble, and, by this hand,
150   she falls me thus about my neck—

OTHELLO: Crying, "O dear Cassio!" as it were; his gesture
    imports it.

CASSIO: So hangs and lolls and weeps upon me; so hales and
    pulls me. Ha, ha, ha!

155 OTHELLO: Now he tells how she plucked him to my chamber.
    O, I see that nose of yours, but not that dog I shall throw
    it to.   *Enter Bianca.*

CASSIO: Well, I must leave her company.

IAGO: Before me! look where she comes.

160 CASSIO: 'Tis such another fitchew![17] marry, a perfumed one.
       What do you mean by this haunting of me?

BIANCA: Let the devil and his dam haunt you! What did you
    mean by that same handkerchief you gave me even now? I
    was a fine fool to take it. I must take out the work? A likely
165   piece of work that you should find it in your chamber and
    not know who left it there! This is some minx's token, and
    I must take out the work? There, give it your hobby-horse.
    Wheresoever you had it, I'll take out no work on't.

CASSIO: How now, my sweet Bianca! how now! how now!

170 OTHELLO: By heaven, that should be my handkerchief!

BIANCA: An you'll come to supper tonight, you may; an you will
    not, come when you are next prepared for.   *Exit.*

IAGO: After her, after her.

CASSIO: Faith, I must; she'll rail i' the street else.

175 IAGO: Will you sup there?

CASSIO: Faith, I intend so.

IAGO: Well, I may chance to see you, for I would very fain
    speak with you.

CASSIO: Prithee, come; will you?

180 IAGO: Go to; say no more.   *Exit Cassio.*

OTHELLO: How shall I murder him, Iago?

IAGO: Did you perceive how he laughed at his vice?

[17]*polecat [a vulgar term for a woman]*

OTHELLO: O Iago!

IAGO: And did you see the handkerchief?

185 OTHELLO: Was that mine?

IAGO: Yours, by this hand. And to see how he prizes the fool-ish woman your wife! She gave it him, and he hath given it his whore.

OTHELLO: I would have him nine years akilling. A fine

190 woman! a fair woman! a sweet woman!

IAGO: Nay, you must forget that.

OTHELLO: Ay, let her rot, and perish, and be damned tonight, for she shall not live. No, my heart is turned to stone; I strike it, and it hurts my hand. O, the world hath not a

195 sweeter creature. She might lie by an emperor's side, and command him tasks.

IAGO: Nay, that's not your way.

OTHELLO: Hang her! I do but say what she is. So delicate with her needle, an admirable musician. O, she will sing the

200 savageness out of a bear. Of so high and plenteous wit and invention!

IAGO: She's the worse for all this.

OTHELLO: O, a thousand, a thousand times. And then, of so gentle a condition!

205 IAGO: Ay, too gentle.

OTHELLO: Nay, that's certain. But yet the pity of it, Iago! O Iago, the pity of it, Iago!

IAGO: If you are so fond over her iniquity, give her patent[18] to offend, for, if it touch not you, it comes near nobody.

210 OTHELLO: I will chop her into messes. Cuckold me!

IAGO: O, 'tis foul in her.

OTHELLO: With mine officer!

IAGO: That's fouler.

OTHELLO: Get me some poison, Iago, this night. I'll not expos-

215 tulate with her, lest her body and beauty unprovide my mind again. This night, Iago:

IAGO: Do it not with poison, strangle her in her bed, even the bed she hath contaminated.

OTHELLO: Good, good, the justice of it pleases, very good.

220 IAGO: And for Cassio, let me be his undertaker. You shall hear more by midnight.

Enter Lodovico, Desdemona, and Attendants.

[18]*license*

OTHELLO: Excellent good. *A trumpet without.* What trumpet is
    that same?

IAGO: Something from Venice, sure. 'Tis Lodovico
225   Come from the Duke. And, see your wife is with him.

LODOVICO: God save the worthy general!

OTHELLO: With all my heart, sir.

LODOVICO: The Duke and Senators of Venice greet you.

OTHELLO: I kiss the instrument of their pleasures.

230 DESD: And what's the news, good cousin Lodovico?

IAGO: I am very glad to see you, signior; Welcome to Cyprus.

LODOVICO: I thank you. How does Lieutenant Cassio?

IAGO: Lives, sir.

DESD: Cousin, there's fall'n between him and my lord
235   An unkind breech; but you shall make all well.

OTHELLO: Are you sure of that?

DESD: My lord?

OTHELLO: "This fail you not to do, as you will"—

LODOVICO: He did not call; he's busy in the paper.
240   Is there division 'twixt my lord and Cassio?

DESD: A most unhappy one. I would do much
    To atone them, for the love I bear to Cassio.

OTHELLO: Fire and brimstone!

DESD: My lord?

245 OTHELLO: Are you wise?

DESD: What, is he angry?

LODOVICO: May be the letter moved him;
    For, as I think, they do command him home,
    Deputing Cassio in his government.

250 DESD: By my troth, I am glad on't.

OTHELLO: Indeed!

DESD: My lord?

OTHELLO: I am glad to see you mad.

DESD: Why, sweet Othello?

255 OTHELLO: Devil! *[Strikes her.]*

DESD: I have not deserved this.

LODOVICO: My lord, this would not be believed in Venice,
    Though I should swear I saw't. 'Tis very much:
    Make her amends; she weeps.

260 OTHELLO: O devil, devil!
    If that the earth could teem with woman's tears,

[19] *[Crocodiles are supposed to shed false tears.]*

      Each drop she falls would prove a crocodile.[19]
        Out of my sight!

DESD: I will not stay to offend you.

265 LODOVICO: Truly, an obedient lady:
        I do beseech your lordship, call her back.

OTHELLO: Mistress!

DESD: My lord?

OTHELLO: What would you with her, sir?

270 LODOVICO: Who, I, my lord?

OTHELLO: Ay, you did wish that I would make her turn:
        Sir, she can turn and turn, and yet go on,
        And turn again; and she can weep, sir, weep;
        And she's obedient, as you say, obedient,

275   Very obedient. Proceed you in your tears.
        Concerning this, sir—O well-painted passion!—
        I am commanded home. Get you away;
        I'll send for you anon. Sir, I obey the mandate,
        And will return to Venice. Hence, avaunt!

280   Cassio shall have my place. And, sir, tonight,
        I do entreat that we may sup together.
        You are welcome, sir, to Cyprus. Goats and monkeys!

                               Exit.

LODOVICO: Is this the noble Moor whom our full Senate
        Call all in all sufficient? This the nature

285   Whom passion could not shake? whose solid virtue
        The shot of accident nor dart of chance
        Could neither graze nor pierce?

IAGO: He is much changed.

LODOVICO: Are his wits safe? Is he not light of brain?

290 IAGO: He's that he is. I may not breathe my censure
        What he might be: if what he might he is not,
        I would to heaven he were!

LODOVICO: What, strike his wife!

295 IAGO: Faith, that was not so well; yet would I knew
        That stroke would prove the worst!

LODOVICO: Is it his use?
        Or did the letters work upon his blood,
        And new create this fault?

300 IAGO: Alas, alas!
        It is not honesty in me to speak
        What I have seen and known. You shall observe him,

And his own courses will denote him so
That I may save my speech: do but go after,
305   And mark how he continues.
Lodovico: I am sorry that I am deceived in him.

Exeunt.

[SCENE II]
[A room in the castle.]

Enter Othello and Emilia.

Othello: You have seen nothing, then?
Emilia: Nor ever heard, nor ever did suspect.
Othello: Yes, you have seen Cassio and she together.
Emilia: But then I saw no harm, and then I heard
5   Each syllable that breath made up between them.
Othello: What, did they never whisper?
Emilia: Never, my lord.
Othello: Nor send you out o' the way?
Emilia: Never.
10 Othello: To fetch her fan, her gloves, her mask, nor nothing?
Emilia: Never, my lord.
Othello: That's strange.
Emilia: I durst, my lord, to wager she is honest,
    Lay down my soul at stake. If you think other,
15   Remove your thought; it doth abuse your bosom.
    If any wretch have put this in your head,
    Let heaven requite it with the serpent's curse!
    For if she be not honest, chaste, and true,
    There's no man happy; the purest of their wives
20   Is foul as slander.
Othello: Bid her come hither; go.   *Exit Emilia.*
    She says enough; yet she's a simple bawd
    That cannot say as much. This is a subtle whore,
    A closet lock and key of villainous secrets:
25   And yet she'll kneel and pray; I have seen her do't.

Enter Desdemona and Emilia.

DESD: My lord, what is your will?

OTHELLO: Pray, chuck, come hither.

DESD: What is your pleasure?

OTHELLO: Let me see your eyes; Look in my face.

30 DESD: What horrible fancy's this?

OTHELLO: *[To Emilia.]* Some of your function,[20] mistress,
    Leave procreants[21] alone and shut the door;
    Cough, or cry "hem," if anybody come:
    Your mystery, your mystery;[22] nay, dispatch.

                             Exit Emilia.

35 DESD: Upon my knees, what doth your speech import?
    I understand a fury in your words,
    But not the words.

OTHELLO: Why, what art thou?

DESD: Your wife, my lord, your true and loyal wife.

40 OTHELLO: Come, swear it, damn thyself;
    Lest, being like one of heaven, the devils themselves
    Should fear to seize thee. Therefore be doubledamn'd;
    Swear thou art honest.

DESD: Heaven doth truly know it.

45 OTHELLO: Heaven truly knows that thou art false as hell.

DESD: To whom, my lord? with whom? how am I false?

OTHELLO: O Desdemona! Away! away! away!

DESD: Alas the heavy day! Why do you weep?
    Am I the motive of these tears, my lord?

50   If haply you my father do suspect
    An instrument of this your calling back,
    Lay not your blame on me. If you have lost him:
    Why, I have lost him too.

OTHELLO: Had it pleased heaven

55   To try me with affliction; had they rain'd
    All kinds of sores and shames on my bare head,
    Steep'd me in poverty to the very lips,
    Given to captivity me and my utmost hopes,
    I should have found in some place of my soul

60   A drop of patience; but, alas, to make me
    A fixed figure for the time of scorn
    To point his slow unmoving finger at!
    Yet could I bear that too, well, very well;
    But there, where I have garner'd[23] up my heart,

[20]*job*

[21]*lovers*

[22]*trade*

[23]*stored*

65　　Where either I must live or bear no life;
　　　The fountain from the which my current runs,
　　　Or else dries up; to be discarded thence!
　　　Or keep it as a cistern for foul toads
　　　To knot and gender in! Turn thy complexion there,
70　　Patience, thou young and roselipp'd cherubin,
　　　Ay, there, look grim as hell!
　DESD: I hope my noble lord esteems me honest.
　OTHELLO: O, ay, as summer flies are in the shambles,[24]
　　　That quicken even with blowing. O thou weed,
75　　Who art so lovely fair and smell'st so sweet
　　　That the sense aches at thee, would thou hadst ne'er been
　　　　　born!
　DESD: Alas, what ignorant sin have I committed?
　OTHELLO: Was this fair paper, this most goodly book,
80　　Made to write "whore" upon? What committed?
　　　Committed! O thou public commoner!
　　　I should make very forges of my cheeks,
　　　That would to cinders burn up modesty,
　　　Did I but speak thy deeds. What committed!
85　　Heaven stops the nose at it, and the moon winks;
　　　The bawdy wind, that kisses all it meets,
　　　Is hush'd within the hollow mine of earth,
　　　And will not hear it. What committed.
　　　Impudent strumpet!
90　DESD: By heaven, you do me wrong.
　OTHELLO: Are not you a strumpet?
　DESD: No, as I am a Christian.
　　　If to preserve this vessel for my lord
　　　From any other foul unlawful touch
95　　Be not to be a strumpet, I am none.
　OTHELLO: What, not a whore?
　DESD: No, as I shall be saved.
　OTHELLO: Is't possible?
　DESD: O, heaven forgive us!
100　OTHELLO: I cry you mercy then;
　　　I took you for that cunning whore of Venice
　　　That married with Othello. You, mistress,
　　　That have the office opposite to Saint Peter,
　　　And keep the gate of hell!

[24]*slaughterhouse*

Enter Emilia.

105   You, you, ay, you!
       We have done our course; there's money for your pains:
       I pray you, turn the key, and keep our counsel.   *Exit.*
   EMILIA: Alas, what does this gentleman conceive?
       How do you, madam? How do you, my good lady?
110 DESD: Faith, half asleep.
   EMILIA: Good madam, what's the matter with my lord?
   DESD: With who?
   EMILIA: Why, with my lord, madam.
   DESD: Who is thy lord?
115 EMILIA: He that is yours, sweet lady.
   DESD: I have none. Do not talk to me, Emilia;
       I cannot weep, nor answer have I none
       But what should go by water. Prithee, tonight
       Lay on my bed my wedding sheets. Remember;
120   And call thy husband hither.
   EMILIA: Here's a change indeed!   *Exit.*
   DESD: 'Tis meet I should be used so, very meet.
       How have I been behaved, that he might stick
       The small'st opinion on my least misuse?

Enter Iago with Emilia.

125 IAGO: What is your pleasure, madam? How is't with you?
   DESD: I cannot tell. Those that do teach young babes
       Do it with gentle means and easy tasks:
       He might have chid me so, for in good faith,
       I am a child to chiding.
130 IAGO: What's the matter, lady?
   EMILIA: Alas, Iago, my lord hath so bewhored her,
       Thrown such despite and heavy terms upon her,
       As true hearts cannot bear.
   DESD: Am I that name, Iago?
135 IAGO: What name, fair lady?
   DESD: Such as she says my lord did say I was.
   EMILIA: He call'd her whore; a beggar in his drink
       Could not have laid such terms upon his callet.[25]
   IAGO: Why did he so?
140 DESD: I do not know; I am sure I am none such.

[25] *whore*

IAGO: Do not weep, do not weep. Alas the day!
EMILIA: Hath she forsook so many noble matches,
   Her father and her country and her friends,
   To be call'd whore? Would it not make one weep?
145 DESD: It is my wretched fortune.
IAGO: How comes this trick upon him?
DESD: Nay, heaven doth know.
EMILIA: I will be hang'd, if some eternal villain,
   Some busy and insinuating rogue,
150   Some cogging cozening[26] slave, to get some office,
   Have not devised this slander; I'll be hang'd else.
IAGO: Fie, there is no such man; it is impossible.
DESD: If any such there be, heaven pardon him!
EMILIA: A halter[27] pardon him! And hell gnaw his bones!
155   Why should he call her whore? Who keeps her company?
   What place? What time? What form? What likelihood?
   The Moor's abused by some most villainous knave,
   Some base notorious knave, some scurvy fellow.
   O heaven, that such companions thou'ldst unfold,[28]
160   And put in every honest hand a whip
   To lash the rascals naked through the world
   Even from the east to the west!
IAGO: Speak within door.[29]
EMILIA: O, fie upon them! Some such squire he was
165   That turn'd your wit the seamy side without,
   And made you to suspect me with the Moor.
IAGO: You are a fool; go to.
DESD: O good Iago,
   What shall I do to win my lord again?
170   Good friend, go to him, for by this light of heaven,
   I know not how I lost him. Here I kneel:
   If e'er my will did trespass 'gainst his love
   Either in discourse of thought or actual deed,
   Or that mine eyes, mine ears, or any sense,
175   Delighted them in any other form,
   Or that I do not yet, and ever did,
   And ever will, though he do shake me off
   To beggarly divorcement, love him dearly,
   Comfort forswear me! Unkindness may do much,
180   And his unkindness may defeat my life,

[26] *deceiving, cheating*

[27] *hanging rope*

[28] *reveal*

[29] *lower your voice*

But never taint my love. I cannot say "whore."
It doth abhor me now I speak the word;
To do the act that might the addition earn
Not the world's mass of vanity could make me.

185   IAGO: I pray you, be content; 'tis but his humor:
The business of the state does him offense,
And he does chide with you.

DESD: If 'twere no other—

IAGO: 'Tis but so, I warrant.   *[Trumpets without.]*

190   Hark, how these instruments summon to supper!
The messengers of Venice stay the meat:
Go in, and weep not; all things shall be well.

Exit women.

Enter Roderigo.

How now, Roderigo!

ROD: I do not find that thou dealest justly with me.

195   IAGO: What in the contrary?

ROD: Every day thou daffest[30] me with some device, Iago;
and rather, as it seems to me now, keepest from me all
conveniency than suppliest me with the least advantage
of hope. I will indeed no longer endure it; nor am I yet

200   persuaded to put up in peace what already I have foolishly
suffered.

IAGO: Will you hear me, Roderigo?

ROD: Faith, I have heard too much, for your words and per-
formances are no kin together.

205   IAGO: You charge me most unjustly.

ROD: With nought but truth. I have wasted myself out of my
means. The jewels you have had from me to deliver to
Desdemona would half have corrupted a votarist.[31] You
have told me she hath received them and returned me

210   expectations and comforts of sudden respect and acquain-
tance; but I find none.

IAGO: Well, go to, very well.

ROD: Very well! go to! I cannot go to, man; nor 'tis not very
well. By this hand, I say 'tis very scurvy, and begin to find

215   myself fopped[32] in it.

IAGO: Very well.

ROD: I tell you 'tis not very well. I will make myself known to

[30]*put me off*

[31]*nun*

[32]*cheated*

Desdemona: If she will return me my jewels, I will give over
my suit and repent my unlawful solicitation; if not, assure
220   yourself I will seek satisfaction of you.

IAGO: You have said now.

ROD: Ay, and said nothing but what I protest intendment of
doing.

IAGO: Why, now I see there's mettle in thee; and even from this
225   instant do build on thee a better opinion than ever before.
Give me thy hand, Roderigo. Thou hast taken against me
a most just exception; but yet, I protest, have dealt most
directly in thy affair.

ROD: It hath not appeared.

230 IAGO: I grant indeed it hath not appeared, and your suspicion is
not without wit and judgement. But, Roderigo, if thou hast
that in thee indeed, which I have greater reason to believe
now than ever, I mean purpose, courage, and valor, this
night show it; if thou the next night following enjoy not
235   Desdemona, take me from this world with treachery and
devise engines[33] for my life.

ROD: Well, what is it? Is it within reason and compass?

IAGO: Sir, there is especial commission come from Venice to
depute Cassio in Othello's place.

240 ROD: Is that true? Why, then Othello and Desdemona return
again to Venice.

IAGO: O, no; he goes into Mauritania, and takes away with him
the fair Desdemona, unless his abode be lingered[34] here by
some accident; wherein none can be so determinate[35] as the
245   removing of Cassio.

ROD: How do you mean, removing of him?

IAGO: Why, by making him uncapable of Othello's place;
knocking out his brains.

ROD: And that you would have me to do?

250 IAGO: Ay, if you dare do yourself a profit and a right. He sups
tonight with a harlotry, and thither will I go to him. He
knows not yet of his honorable fortune. If you will watch
his going thence, which his will fashion to fall out between
twelve and one, you may take him at your pleasure; I will
255   be near to second your attempt, and he shall fall between
us. Come, stand not amazed at it, but go along with me; I
will show you such a necessity in his death that you shall

[33]*plans*

[34]*extended*

[35]*guaranteeing*

think yourself bound to put it on him. It is now high sup-
pertime, and the night grows to waste. About it.

260 ROD: I will hear further reason for this.

IAGO: And you shall be satisfied.

Exeunt.

[SCENE III]
[Another room in the castle.]

Enter Othello, Desdemona, Lodovico, Emilia, and Attendants.

LODOVICO: I do beseech you, sir, trouble yourself no further.

OTHELLO: O, pardon me; 'twill do me good to walk.

LODOVICO: Madam, good night; I humbly thank your
ladyship.

5 DESD: Your honor is most welcome.

OTHELLO: Will you walk, sir? O—Desdemona—

DESD: My lord?

OTHELLO: Get you to bed on the instant; I will be returned
forthwith: Dismiss your attendant there; look it be done.
Exeunt [Othello, Lodovico, and Attendants.]

10 DESD: I will, my lord.

EMILIA: How goes it now? He looks gentler than he did.

DESD: He says he will return incontinent:[36]
He hath commanded me to go to bed,
And bade me to dismiss you.

15 EMILIA: Dismiss me?

DESD: It was his bidding; therefore, good Emilia,
Give me my nightly wearing, and adieu.
We must not now displease him.

EMILIA: I would you had never seen him!

20 DESD: So would not I. My love doth so approve him,
That even his stubbornness, his checks, his frowns—
Prithee, unpin me—have grace and favor in them.

EMILIA: I have laid those sheets you bade me on the bed.

DESD: All's one. Good faith, how foolish are our minds!

25   If I do die before thee, prithee shroud me

[36]*immediately*

In one of those same sheets.
EMILIA: Come, come, you talk.
DESD: My mother had a maid call'd Barbara;
  She was in love, and he she loved proved mad
30 And did forsake her. She had a song of "willow";
  An old thing 'twas, but it express'd her fortune,
  And she died singing it. That song tonight
  Will not go from my mind; I have much to do,
  But to go hang my head all at one side
35 And sing it like poor Barbara. Prithee, dispatch.[37]
EMILIA: Shall I go fetch your nightgown?
DESD: No, unpin me here.
  This Lodovico is a proper man.
EMILIA: A very handsome man.
40 DESD: He speaks well.
EMILIA: I know a lady in Venice would have walked barefoot to
  Palestine for a touch of his nether lip.
DESD: *[Sings.]* "The poor soul sat sighing by a sycamore tree,
        Sing all a green willow;
45   Her hand on her bosom, her head on her knee,
          Sing willow, willow, willow.
      The fresh streams ran by her, and murmur'd her moans;
          Sing willow, willow, willow;
      Her salt tears fell from her, and soften'd the stones"—
50   Lay by these:—
          Sing willow, willow, willow"
  Prithee, hie thee; he'll come anon:—
          Sing all a green willow must be my garland.
      Let nobody blame him; his scorn I approve
55 Nay, that's not next. Hark, who is't that knocks?
EMILIA: It's the wind.
DESD: *[Sings.]* I call'd my love false love; but what said he then?
          Sing willow, willow, willow:
      If I court moe women, you'll couch with moe men
60 So get thee gone; good night. Mine eyes do itch;
  Doth that bode weeping?
EMILIA: 'Tis neither here nor there.
DESD: I have heard it said so. O, these men, these men!
  Dost thou in conscience think—tell me, Emilia—
65 That there be women do abuse their husbands

[37]*be quick*

In such gross kind?

EMILIA: There be some such, no question.

DESD: Wouldst thou do such a deed for all the world?

EMILIA: Why, would not you?

70 DESD: No, by this heavenly light!

EMILIA: Nor I neither by this heavenly light; I might do't as well i' the dark.

DESD: Wouldst thou do such a thing for all the world?

EMILIA: The world's a huge thing; it is a great price[38]

75   For a final vice.

DESD: In troth, I think thou wouldst not.

EMILIA: In troth, I think I should, and undo't when I had done. Marry, I would not do such a thing for a joint-ring,[39] nor for measures of lawn,[40] nor for gowns, petticoats, nor

80   caps, nor any petty exhibition;[41] but, for the whole world why, who would not make her husband a cuckold to make him a monarch? I should venture purgatory for't.

DESD: Beshrew me, if I would do such a wrong For the whole world.

85 EMILIA: Why, the wrong is but a wrong i' the world; and having the world for your labor, 'tis a wrong in your own world, and you might quickly make it right.

DESD: I do not think there is any such woman.

EMILIA: Yes, a dozen, and as many to the vantage[42] as would

90   store the world they played for.[43]

But I do think it is their husbands' faults
If wives do fall; say that they slack their duties
And pour our treasures into foreign laps,
Or else break out in peevish jealousies,

95   Throwing restraint upon us, or say they strike us,
Or scant our former having in despite,[44]
Why, we have galls, and though we have some grace,
Yet have we some revenge. Let husbands know
Their wives have sense like them; they see and smell

100   And have their palates both for sweet and sour,
As husbands have. What is it that they do
When they change us for others? Is it sport?
I think it is. And doth affection breed it?
I think it doth. Is't frailty that thus errs?

105   It is so too. And have not we affections,

[38]prize

[39]small token of love

[40]fine linen

[41]small show of wealth

[42]enough besides

[43]to populate the whole world

[44]withhold our allowance out of spite

Desires for sport, and frailty, as men have?
Then let them use us well; else let them know,
The ills we do, their ills instruct us so.
DESD: Good night, good night. Heaven me such uses send,
110   Not to pick bad from bad, but by bad mend!

Exeunt.

ACT V

[SCENE I]
[Cyprus. A street.]

Enter Iago and Roderigo.

IAGO: Here, stand behind this bulk; straight will he come:
    Wear thy good rapier[1] bare, and put it home.
    Quick, quick; fear nothing; I'll be at thy elbow.
    It makes us, or it mars us; think on that,
5   And fix most firm thy resolution.
ROD: Be near at hand; I may miscarry[2] in't.
IAGO: Here, at thy hand, be bold, and take thy stand.
    [Retires.]
ROD: I have no great devotion to the deed;
10   And yet he hath given me satisfying reasons:
    'Tis but a man gone. Forth, my sword; he dies.
IAGO: I have rubb'd this young quat[3] almost to the sense,[4]
    And he grows angry. Now, whether he kill Cassio,
    Or Cassio him, or each do kill the other,
15   Every way makes my gain. Live Roderigo,
    He calls me to a restitution[5] large
    Of gold and jewels that I bobb'd[6] from him,
    As gifts to Desdemona;
    It must not be. If Cassio do remain,
    He hath a daily beauty in his life
20   That makes me ugly; and besides, the Moor
    May unfold me to him; there stand I in much peril:
    No, he must die. Be't so. I hear him coming.

Enter Cassio.

ROD: I know his gait; 'tis he. Villain, thou diest!

---

[1] *dagger*

[2] *fail*

[3] *pimple*

[4] *quick*

[5] *repayment*

[6] *stole*

CASSIO: That thrust had been mine enemy indeed,
　　　But that my coat is better than thou know'st;
25　　I will make proof of thine.
ROD: O, I am slain!
　　　　[Iago from behind wounds Cassio in the leg, and exit.]
CASSIO: I am maim'd forever. Help, ho! Murder! Murder!

Enter Othello.

OTHELLO: The voice of Cassio; Iago keeps his word.
ROD: O, villain that I am!
30　OTHELLO: It is even so.
CASSIO: O, help, ho! Light! A surgeon!
OTHELLO: 'Tis he. O brave Iago, honest and just,
　　　That hast such noble sense of thy friend's wrong!
　　　Thou teachest me. Minion, your dear lies dead,
35　　And your unblest fate hies. Strumpet, I come!
　　　Forth of my heart those charms, thine eyes, are blotted;
　　　Thy bed, lust-stain'd shall with lust's blood be spotted.

　　　　　　　　　　　　　　　　　　Exit.

Enter Lodovico and Gratiano.

CASSIO: What, ho! No watch? No passage? Murder! Murder!
GRATIANO: 'Tis some mischance;[7] the cry is very direful.
40　CASSIO: O, help!
LODOVICO: Hark!
ROD: O wretched villain!
LODOVICO: Two or three groan; it is a heavy night:
　　　These may be counterfeits;[8] let's think't unsafe
45　　To come in to the cry without more help.
ROD: Nobody come? Then shall I bleed to death.

Enter Iago, with a light.

LODOVICO: Hark!
GRATIANO: Here's one comes in his shirt, with light and
　　　weapons.
50　IAGO: Who's there? Whose noise is this that cries on murder?

[7]*disaster*

[8]*traps*

LODOVICO: We do not know.

IAGO: Did not you hear a cry?

CASSIO: Here, here! for heaven's sake, help me!

IAGO: What's the matter?

55 GRATIANO: This is Othello's ancient, as I take it.

LODOVICO: The same indeed; a very valiant fellow.

IAGO: What are you here that cry so grievously?

CASSIO: Iago? O, I am spoil'd, undone by villains!
   Give me some help.

60 IAGO: O me, lieutenant! What villains have done this?

CASSIO: I think that one of them is hereabout,
   And cannot make away.

IAGO: O treacherous villains!
   What are you there? Come in and give some help.

65 ROD: O, help me here!

CASSIO: That's one of them.

IAGO: O murderous slave! O villain!

ROD: O damn'd Iago! O inhuman dog!

IAGO: Kill men i' the dark! Where be these bloody thieves?

70   How silent is this town! Ho! Murder! Murder!
   What may you be? Are you of good or evil?

LODOVICO: As you shall prove⁹ us, praise¹⁰ us.

IAGO: Signior Lodovico?

LODOVICO: He, sir.

75 IAGO: I cry you mercy. Here's Cassio hurt by villains.

GRATIANO: Cassio?

IAGO: How is't, brother?

CASSIO: My leg is cut in two.

IAGO: Marry, heaven forbid!

80   Light, gentlemen; I'll bind it with my shirt.

Enter Bianca.

BIANCA: What is the matter, ho? Who is't that cried?

IAGO: Who is't that cried!

BIANCA: O my dear Cassio, my sweet Cassio! O Cassio, Cassio,
   Cassio!

85 IAGO: O notable strumpet! Cassio, may you suspect
   Who they should be that have thus mangled you?

CASSIO: No.

⁹*find*

¹⁰*appraise, value*

GRATIANO: I am sorry to find you thus; I have been to seek
    you.

[90] IAGO: Lend me a garter.[11] So. O, for a chair,
    To bear him easily hence!

BIANCA: Alas, he faints! O Cassio, Cassio, Cassio!

IAGO: Gentlemen all, I do suspect this trash
    To be a party in this injury.

[95]   Patience awhile, good Cassio. Come, come;
    Lend me a light. Know we this face or no?
    Alas, my friend and my dear countryman
    Roderigo? No—yes, sure. O heaven! Roderigo.

GRATIANO: What, of Venice?

[100] IAGO: Even he, sir. Did you know him?

GRATIANO: Know him! ay.

IAGO: Signior Gratiano? I cry you gentle pardon;
    These bloody accidents must excuse my manners,
    That so neglected you.

[105] GRATIANO: I am glad to see you.

IAGO: How do you, Cassio? O, a chair, a chair!

GRATIANO: Roderigo!

IAGO: He, he, 'tis he. O, that's well said: the chair.
    Some good man bear him carefully from hence;
[110]   I'll fetch the general's surgeon.
    For you, mistress,
    Save you your labor. He that lies slain here, Cassio,
    Was my dear friend; what malice was between you?

CASSIO: None in the world; nor do I know the man.

[115] IAGO: What, look you pale? O, bear him out o' the air.
    Stay you, good gentlemen. Look you pale, mistress?
    Do you perceive the gastness[12] of her eye?
    Nay, if you stare, we shall hear more anon.
    Behold her well; I pray you, look upon her.
[120]   Do you see, gentlemen? Nay, guiltiness will speak,
    Though tongues were out of use.

Enter Emilia.

EMILIA: 'Las, what's the matter? What's the matter, husband?

IAGO: Cassio hath here been set on in the dark

125   By Roderigo, and fellows that are 'scaped;
        He's almost slain, and Roderigo dead.
    EMILIA: Alas, good gentleman! alas, good Cassio!
    IAGO: This is the fruit of whoring. Prithee, Emilia,
        Go know of Cassio where he supp'd tonight.
130   What, do you shake at that?
    BIANCA: He supp'd at my house; but I therefore shake not.
    IAGO: O, did he so? I charge you, go with me.
    EMILIA: Fie, fie upon thee, strumpet!
    BIANCA: I am no strumpet, but of life as honest
135   As you that thus abuse me.
    EMILIA: As I! foh! fie upon thee!
    IAGO: Kind gentlemen, let's go see poor Cassio dress'd.
        Come, mistress, you must tell's another tale.
        Emilia, run you to the citadel,
140   And tell my lord and lady what hath happ'd!
        Will you go on? *[Aside.]* This is the night
        That either makes me or fordoes me quite.

                                            Exeunt.

                        [SCENE II]
                [A bedchamber in the castle.]
            Desdemona in bed asleep; a light burning.

Enter Othello.

OTHELLO: It is the cause, it is the cause, my soul.
        Let me not name it to you, you chaste stars!
        It is the cause. Yet I'll not shed her blood,
        Nor scar that whiter skin of hers than snow
5   And smooth as monumental alabaster.
        Yet she must die, else she'll betray more men.
        Put out the light, and then put out the light.
        If I quench thee, thou flaming minister,
        I can again thy former light restore,
10   Should I repent me; but once put out thy light,

¹³*essence of life*
[Prometheus was
a mythical figure
who stole fire
from the gods and
gave it to man.]

¹⁴*relight*

Thou cunning'st pattern of excelling nature,
I know not where is that Promethean heat[13]
That can thy light relume.[14] When I have pluck'd the rose,
I cannot give it vital growth again,

15   It must needs wither; I'll smell it on the tree. *[Kisses her.]*
O, balmy breath, that dost almost persuade
Justice to break her sword! One more, one more;
Be thus when thou art dead, and I will kill thee,
And love thee after. One more, and this the last:

20   So sweet was ne'er so fatal. I must weep,
But they are cruel tears; this sorrow's heavenly,
It strikes where it doth love. She wakes.

DESD: Who's there? Othello?

OTHELLO: Ay, Desdemona.

25 DESD: Will you come to bed, my lord?

OTHELLO: Have you pray'd tonight, Desdemona?

DESD: Ay, my lord.

OTHELLO: If you bethink yourself of any crime
Unreconciled as yet to heaven and grace,

¹⁵*ask forgiveness*

30   Solicit[15] for it straight.

DESD: Alas, my lord, what may you mean by that?

OTHELLO: Well, do it, and be brief; I will walk by:
I would not kill thy unprepared spirit;

¹⁶*forbid*

No, heaven forfend![16] I would not kill thy soul.

35 DESD: Talk you of killing?

OTHELLO: Ay, I do.

DESD: Then heaven have mercy on me!

OTHELLO: Amen, with all my heart!

DESD: If you say so, I hope you will not kill me.

40 OTHELLO: Hum!

DESD: And yet I fear you, for you are fatal then
When your eyes roll so. Why I should fear I know not,
Since guiltiness I know not; but yet I feel I fear.

OTHELLO: Think on thy sins.

45 DESD: They are loves I bear to you.

OTHELLO: Ay, and for that thou diest.

DESD: That death's unnatural that kills for loving.
Alas, why gnaw you so your nether lip?
Some bloody passion shakes your very frame:

50   These are portents; but yet I hope, I hope,

They do not point on me.

OTHELLO: Peace, and be still!

DESD: I will so. What's the matter?

OTHELLO: That handkerchief which I so loved and gave thee
55   Thou gavest to Cassio.

DESD: No, by my life and soul!
     Send for the man, and ask him.

OTHELLO: Sweet soul, take heed,
     Take heed of perjury; thou are on thy deathbed.
60 DESD: Ay, but not yet to die.

OTHELLO: Yes, presently:
     Therefore confess thee freely of thy sin;
     For to deny each article with oath
     Cannot remove nor choke the strong conception
65   That I do groan withal.[17] Thou art to die.

DESD: Then Lord have mercy on me!

OTHELLO: I say, amen.

DESD: And have you mercy too! I never did
     Offend you in my life; never loved Cassio
70   But with such general warranty of heaven
     As I might love. I never gave him token.

OTHELLO: By heaven, I saw my handkerchief in 's hand.
     O perjured woman! Thou dost stone my heart,
     And makest me call what I intend to do
75   A murder, which I thought a sacrifice:
     I saw the handkerchief.

DESD: He found it then;
     I never gave it him. Send for him hither;
     Let him confess a truth.
80 OTHELLO: He hath confess'd.

DESD: What, my lord?

OTHELLO: That he hath used thee.

DESD: How? unlawfully?

OTHELLO: Ay.
85 DESD: He will not say so.

OTHELLO: No, his mouth is stopp'd;
     Honest Iago hath ta'en order for't.

DESD: O, my fear interprets! What, is he dead?

OTHELLO: Had all his hairs been lives, my great revenge
90   Had stomach for them all.

[17]*with*

DESD: Alas, he is betray'd, and I undone!

OTHELLO: Out, strumpet! Weep'st thou for him to my face?

DESD: O, banish me, my lord, but kill me not!

OTHELLO: Down, strumpet!

95   DESD: Kill me tomorrow; let me live tonight!

OTHELLO: Nay, if you strive—

DESD: But half an hour!

OTHELLO: Being done, there is no pause.

DESD: But while I say one prayer!

100   OTHELLO: It is too late. *[He smothers her.]*

EMILIA: *Without.* My lord, my lord! What, ho! my lord, my
    lord!

OTHELLO: What noise is this? Not dead? not yet quite dead?
    I that am cruel am yet merciful;

105   I would not have thee linger in thy pain. So, so.

EMILIA: *Without.* What, ho! my lord, my lord!

OTHELLO: Who's there?

EMILIA: *Without.* O, good my lord, I would speak a word
    with you!

110   OTHELLO: Yes, 'tis Emilia. By and by. She's dead.
    'Tis like she comes to speak of Cassio's death.
    The noise was here. Ha! no more moving?
    Still as the grave. Shall she come in? were't good?
    I think she stirs again. No. What's best to do?

115   If she come in, she'll sure speak to my wife.
    My wife! My wife! What wife? I have no wife.
    O, insupportable! O heavy hour!
    Methinks it should be now a huge eclipse
    Of sun and moon, and that the affrighted globe

120   Should yawn[18] at alteration.[19]

EMILIA: *Without.* I do beseech you
    That I may speak with you, O, good my lord!

OTHELLO: I had forgot thee. O, come in, Emilia.
    Soft, by and by. Let me the curtains draw.

125   Where art thou?   *[Unlocks the door.]*

Enter Emilia.

    What's the matter with thee now?

EMILIA: O, my good lord, yonder's foul murders done!

OTHELLO: What, now?

[18]*open, as in an earthquake*

[19]*the change*

EMILIA: But now, my lord.

130 OTHELLO: It is the very error of the moon;
  She comes more nearer earth than she was wont
  And makes men mad.

EMILIA: Cassio, my lord, hath kill'd a young Venetian
  Call'd Roderigo.

135 OTHELLO: Roderigo kill'd?
  And Cassio kill'd?

EMILIA: No, Cassio is not kill'd.

OTHELLO: Not Cassio kill'd! Then murder 's out of tune,
  And sweet revenge grows harsh.

140 DESD: O, falsely, falsely murdered!

EMILIA: Alas, what cry is that?

OTHELLO: That? what?

EMILIA: Out, and alas! That was my lady's voice.
  Help! help, ho! help! O lady, speak again!

145   Sweet Desdemona! O sweet mistress, speak!

DESD: A guiltless death I die.

EMILIA: O, who hath done this deed?

DESD: Nobody; I myself. Farewell;
  Commend me to my kind lord. O, farewell!   *She dies.*

150 OTHELLO: Why, how should she be murdered?

EMILIA: Alas, who knows?

OTHELLO: You heard her say herself, it was not I.

EMILIA: She said so; I must needs report the truth.

OTHELLO: She's like a liar gone to burning hell;

155   'Twas I that kill'd her.

EMILIA: O, the more angel she,
  And you the blacker devil!

OTHELLO: She turn'd to folly, and she was a whore.

EMILIA: Thou dost belie her, and thou art a devil.

160 OTHELLO: She was false as water.

EMILIA: Thou art rash as fire, to say
  That she was false. O, she was heavenly true!

OTHELLO: Cassio did top her; ask thy husband else.
  O, I were damn'd beneath all depth in hell,

165   But that I did proceed upon just grounds
  To this extremity. Thy husband knew it all.

EMILIA: My husband!

OTHELLO: Thy husband.

[20]topaz

EMILIA: That she was false to wedlock?

170 OTHELLO: Ay, with Cassio. Nay, had she been true,
     If heaven would make me such another world
     Of one entire and perfect chrysolite,[20]
     I'ld not have sold her for it.

EMILIA: My husband!

175 OTHELLO: Ay, 'twas he that told me first:
     An honest man he is, and hates the slime
     That sticks on filthy deeds.

EMILIA: My husband?

OTHELLO: What needs this iteration, woman? I say thy
180   husband.

EMILIA: O mistress, villainy hath made mocks with love!
     My husband say that she was false!

OTHELLO: He, woman;
     I say thy husband. Dost understand the word?
185   My friend, thy husband, honest, honest Iago.

EMILIA: If he say so, may his pernicious soul
     Rot half a grain a day! He lies to the heart.
     She was too fond of her most filthy bargain.[21]

[21]her marriage

OTHELLO: Ha!

190 EMILIA: Do thy worst;
     This deed of thine is no more worthy heaven
     Than thou wast worthy her.

OTHELLO: Peace, you were best.

EMILIA: Thou hast not half that power to do me harm
195   As I have to be hurt. O gull! O dolt!
     As ignorant as dirt! Thou hast done a deed—
     I care not for thy sword; I'll make thee known,
     Though I lost twenty lives. Help! help, ho! help!
     The Moor hath kill'd my mistress! Murder, murder!

Enter Montano, Gratiano, Iago, and others.

200 MONTANO: What is the matter? How now, general?

EMILIA: O, are you come, Iago? You have done well,
     That men must lay their murders on your neck.

GRATIANO: What is the matter?

EMILIA: Disprove this villain, if thou be'st a man:
205   He says thou told'st him that his wife was false;

I know thou didst not, thou'rt not such a villain.
Speak, for my heart is full.
IAGO: I told him what I thought, and told no more
Than what he found himself was apt and true.
210   EMILIA: But did you ever tell him she was false?
IAGO: I did.
EMILIA: You told a lie, an odious, damned lie;
Upon my soul, a lie, a wicked lie!
She false with Cassio? Did you say with Cassio?
215   IAGO: With Cassio, mistress. Go to, charm your tongue.
EMILIA: I will not charm my tongue; I am bound to speak.
My mistress here lies murdered in her bed.
ALL: O heavens forfend!
EMILIA: And your reports have set the murder on.
220   OTHELLO: Nay, stare not, masters; it is true indeed.
GRATIANO: 'Tis a strange truth.
MONTANO: O monstrous act!
EMILIA: Villainy, villainy, villainy!
I think upon't, I think, I smell't, O villainy!
225   I thought so then. I'll kill myself for grief:
O villainy, villainy!
IAGO: What, are you mad? I charge you, get you home.
EMILIA: Good gentlemen, let me have leave to speak;
'Tis proper I obey him, but not now.
230   Perchance, Iago, I will ne'er go home.
OTHELLO: O! O! O!   *Othello falls on the bed.*
EMILIA: Nay, lay thee down and roar;
For thou hast kill'd the sweetest innocent
That e'er did lift up eye.
235   OTHELLO: *[Rises.]* O, she was foul!
I scarce did know you, uncle; there lies your niece,
Whose breath indeed these hands have newly stopp'd.
I know this act shows horrible and grim.
GRATIANO: Poor Desdemon! I am glad thy father's dead:
240   Thy match was mortal to him, and pure grief
Shore his old thread in twain; did he live now,
This sight would make him do a desperate turn,
Yea, curse his better angel from his side,
And fall to reprobation.[22]
245   OTHELLO: 'Tis pitiful, but yet Iago knows

[22]*damnation*

[23]*souvenir*

That she with Cassio hath the act of shame
A thousand times committed. Cassio confess'd it,
And she did gratify his amorous works
With that recognizance[23] and pledge of love
250   Which I first gave her. I saw it in his hand:
It was a handkerchief, an antique token
My father gave my mother.
EMILIA: O heaven! O heavenly powers!
IAGO: 'Zounds! Hold your peace.
255 EMILIA: 'Twill out, 'twill. I peace!

[24]*the North wind,*
which blows esp-
cially violently

No, I will speak as liberal as the north;[24]
Let heaven and men and devils, let them all,
All, all, cry shame against me, yet I'll speak.
IAGO: Be wise, and get you home.
260 EMILIA: I will not.
GRATIANO: Fie! Your sword upon a woman?
EMILIA: O thou dull Moor! That handkerchief thou speak'st
of
I found by fortune and did give my husband;
For often with a solemn earnestness,
265   More than indeed belong'd to such a trifle,
He begg'd of me to steal it.
IAGO: Villainous whore!
EMILIA: She give it Cassio? No, alas, I found it,
And I did give't my husband.
270 IAGO: Filth, thou liest!
EMILIA: By heaven, I do not, I do not, gentlemen.
O murderous coxcomb![25] What should such a fool

[25]*fool's cap*

Do with so good a wife?
OTHELLO: Are there not stones in heaven
275   But what serve for thunder? Precious villain!

The Moor [Othello] runs at Iago.
Iago kills his wife.

GRATIANO: The woman falls; sure, he hath kill'd his wife.
EMILIA: Ay, ay! O, lay me by my mistress' side.   *Exit Iago.*
GRATIANO: He's gone, but his wife's kill'd.
MONTANO: 'Tis a notorious villain. Take you this weapon,
280   Which I have here recover'd from the Moor:
Come, guard the door without; let him not pass,
But kill him rather. I'll after that same villain,

For 'tis a damned slave.

Exit Montano and Gratiano.

OTHELLO: I am not valiant neither,
285   But every puny whipster[26] gets my sword.
    But why should honor outlive honesty?
    Let it go all.

EMILIA: What did thy song bode, lady?
    Hark, canst thou hear me? I will play the swan,
290   And die in music.
        [Sings.] Willow, willow, willow.
    Moor, she was chaste; she loved thee, cruel Moor;
    So come my soul to bliss, as I speak true;
    So speaking as I think, I die, I die.   *She dies.*
295 OTHELLO: I have another weapon in this chamber;
    O, here it is. Uncle, I must come forth.

GRATIANO: *[Within.]* If thou attempt it, it will cost thee dear:
    Thou hast no weapon, and perforce must suffer.

OTHELLO: Look in upon me then, and speak with me,
300   Or, naked as I am, I will assault thee.

Enter Gratiano.

GRATIANO: What is the matter?

OTHELLO: Behold, I have a weapon;
    A better never did itself sustain
    Upon a soldier's thigh. I have seen the day
305   That with this little arm and this good sword
    I have made my way through more impediments
    Than twenty times your stop. But, O vain boast!
    Who can control his fate? 'Tis not so now.
    Be not afraid, though you do see me weapon'd;
310   Here is my journey's end, here is my butt
    And very seamark of my utmost sail.
    Do you go back dismay'd? 'Tis a lost fear:
    Man[27] but a rush[28] against Othello's breast,
    And he retires.[29] Where should Othello go?
315   Now, how dost thou look now? O ill-starr'd wench!
    Pale as thy smock! When we shall meet at compt,[30]
    This look of thine will hurl my soul from heaven,
    And fiends will snatch at it. Cold, cold, my girl

[26]*insignificant underling*

[27]*use*

[28]*a weak weed*

[29]*falls*

[30]*the Last Judgment*

Even like thy chastity. O cursed, cursed slave!
320   Whip me, ye devils,
From the possession of this heavenly sight!
Blow me about in winds! Roast me in sulphur!
Wash me in steepdown gulfs of liquid fire!
O Desdemon! dead, Desdemon! dead!
325   O! O! O!

Enter Lodovico, Montano, Iago, and Officers, Cassio in a chair.

Lodovico: Where is this rash and most unfortunate man?
Othello: That's he that was Othello. Here I am.
Lodovico: Where is that viper? Bring the villain forth.
Othello: I look down towards his feet; but that's a fable.
330   If that thou be'st a devil, I cannot kill thee.
Lodovico: Wrench his sword from him.
Iago: I bleed, sir, but not kill'd.
Othello: I am not sorry neither. I'ld have thee live,
For, in my sense, 'tis happiness to die.
335 Lodovico: O thou Othello, that wert once so good,
What shall be said to thee?
Othello: Why, anything;
An honorable murderer, if you will,
For nought did I in hate, but all in honor.
340 Lodovico: This wretch hath part confess'd his villainy.
Did you and he consent in Cassio's death?
Othello: Ay.
Cassio: Dear general, I never gave you cause.
Othello: I do believe it, and I ask your pardon.
345   Will you, I pray, demand that demi-devil
Why he hath thus ensnared my soul and body?
Iago: Demand me nothing; what you know: you know.
From this time forth I never will speak word.
Lodovico: What, not to pray?
350 Gratiano: Torments will ope your lips.
Othello: Well, thou dost best.
Lodovico: Sir, you shall understand what hath befall'n,
Which, as I think, you know not. Here is a letter
Found in the pocket of the slain Roderigo,
355   And here another. The one of them imports

     The death of Cassio to be undertook
     By Roderigo.
OTHELLO: O villain!
CASSIO: Most heathenish and most gross!
360 LODOVICO: Now here's another discontented paper,
     Found in his pocket too; and this, it seems,
     Roderigo meant to have sent this damned villain;
     But that, belike, Iago in the interim
     Came in and satisfied him.
365 OTHELLO: O the pernicious caitiff!
     How came you, Cassio, by that handkerchief
     That was my wife's?
CASSIO: I found it in my chamber;
     And he himself confess'd but even now
370   That there he dropp'd it for a special purpose
     Which wrought to his desire.
OTHELLO: O fool! fool! fool!
CASSIO: There is besides in Roderigo's letter,
     How he upbraids[31] Iago, that he made him
375   Brave me upon the watch, whereon it came
     That I was cast. And even but now he spake
     After long seeming dead, Iago hurt him,
     Iago set him on.
LODOVICO: You must forsake this room, and go with us:
380   Your power and your command is taken off,
     And Cassio rules in Cyprus. For this slave,
     If there be any cunning cruelty
     That can torment him much and hold him long,
     It shall be his. You shall close prisoner rest,
385   Till that the nature of your fault be known
     To the Venetian state. Come, bring away.
OTHELLO: Soft you; a word or two before you go.
     I have done the state some service, and they know't.
     No more of that. I pray you, in your letters,
390   When you shall these unlucky deeds relate,
     Speak of me as I am; nothing extenuate,
     Nor set down aught in malice. Then must you speak
     Of one that loved not wisely but too well;
     Of one not easily jealous, but, being wrought,
395   Perplex'd in the extreme; of one whose hand,

[31] scolds

[32] crying

Like the base Indian, threw a pearl away
Richer than all his tribe; of one whose subdued eyes,
Albeit unused to the melting mood,[32]
Drop tears as fast as the Arabian trees
400   Their medicinal gum. Set you down this;
And say besides, that in Aleppo once,

[33] dishonored

Where a malignant and a turban'd[33] Turk
Beat a Venetian and traduced the state,
I took by the throat the circumcised dog
405   And smote him, thus.   *Stabs himself.*

LODOVICO: O bloody period!
GRATIANO: All that's spoke is marr'd.
OTHELLO: I kiss'd thee ere I kill'd thee. No way but this,
        Killing myself, to die upon a kiss.
410   *He dies.*

CASSIO: This did I fear, but thought he had no weapon;
        For he was great of heart.

[34] [The ancient
Spartans were
famous for their
lack of emotion.]

LODOVICO: O Spartan[34] dog,
        More fell than anguish, hunger, or the sea!
        Look on the tragic loading of this bed;
415   This is thy work. The object poisons sight;
        Let it be hid. Gratiano, keep the house,
        And seize upon the fortunes of the Moor,
        For they succeed on you. To you, Lord Governor,
        Remains the censure of this hellish villain,
420   The time, the place, the torture. O, enforce it!
        Myself will straight aboard, and to the state
        This heavy act with heavy heart relate.

                                            Exeunt.

THE END

VOCABULARY AND GLOSSARY

Act I, Scene I
"**Tush**" – an expression of contempt
"**'Sblood**" – an oath (originally "God's blood!")
suit – appeal
"**Certes**" – "for certain"
"**Forsooth**" – "Indeed"
Rhodes – an island southeast of Greece
Cyprus – an island south of Turkey
knave – rascal, wretched fellow
obsequious – full of flattery
naught – nothing
"**'Zounds**" – an oath ("God's wounds!")
ruffians – hoodlums
lascivious – sexually overactive
saucy – showing a lack of respect
wheeling – freewheeling, rootless

Act I, Scene II
stuff – an essential part
out-tongue – speak louder than
yond – yonder
haste-post-haste – extra-quick
heat – urgency
makes – does

Act I, Scene III
disproportion'd – inconsistent
frank – obvious
aught – anything
preposterously – ridiculously
pith – strength
dearest – most valuable
conjuration – spell
withal – with
wrought – made a change
vouch – swear
overt – obvious
imminent – about to be
breach – space between safe places

Anthropophagi – man-eaters
hitherto – therefore
equivocal – the same
visage – face
consecrate – dedicate to
comply – satisfy
defunct – extinguished
scant – give little attention to
prithee – pray thee
direction – instructions
fond – stupid
betimes – early
knavery – mischief

Act II, Scene I
highwrought – turbulent
expectancy – expectation
arrivance – arrival
allowance – experience
ensteep'd – submerged
footing – arrival
citadel – fort
"fie" – an exclamation of contempt
pate – head
disclose – make known
bark – boat
list – listen
voluble – talkative
prologue – beginning
haply – perhaps
peradventure – perhaps

Act II, Scene II
tidings – news

Act II, Scene III
warrant – guarantee
game – playfulness
brace – pair
fain – gladly
caroused – drunk
equinox – the day of the year in which the hours of night and day are exactly the same; in this case, a counterbalance
hazard – risk

"Diablo" – "Devil" (an oath)
barbarous – savage
odds – argument
censure – judgment
entreats – begs

Act III, Scene I

—

Act III, Scene II

—

Act III, Scene III
strangeness – unfriendliness
poise – importance
ruminate – think
"I'ld" – "I would"
clime – climate
vehement – emotional
government – self-restraint
"Avaunt!" – "Be gone!"
"immortal Jove's dead clamours" – thunderbolts; Jove, king of the gods in Roman
    mythology, was said to be responsible for thunder.
sith – since
"Dian's visage" – the face of Diana, goddess of chastity and purity
aspics' – venomous snakes'
Hellespont – the strait between the Aegean Sea and the Sea of Marmara

Act III, Scene IV
catechize – ask a series of questions; in the Catholic church, a formal series of
    questions, called a catechism, is asked of a person entering the congregation.
humors – According to a theory popular from ancient to Elizabethan times, bodily
    fluids called humors determine a person's mood and character. An excess of
    yellow bile makes a person choleric (angry and vengeful); too much black bile
    results in a melancholy, or depressed, personality; an abundance of phlegm
    (mucus) makes for a sluggish and dull nature, called phlegmatic; and too
    much blood results in a sanguine, or cheerful, type. Here, Desdemona says
    that Othello is so cheerful and easygoing because the sun has drawn off his ill
    humors.
unhatch'd – developing
indicted – charged

Act IV, Scene I
boding – warning
belie – slander
shadowing – foreshadowing
forbear – hold off
lethargy – coma
horned – A cuckold (man cheated on by his wife) is commonly described as having horns.
unproper – shared with someone else
anon – later
spleen – the organ that produces yellow bile, or choler
strumpet – whore
bauble – plaything
dam – mistress
expostulate – argue
"By my troth" – "In truth"
goats and monkeys – animals notorious for their sexual appetites

Act IV, Scene II
complexion – face
cherubin – angel
"thou'ldst" – "thou should"
fopped – duped

Act IV, Scene III
hie – hurry

Act V, Scene I
fordoes – dooms

Act V, Scene II
alabaster – a white stone often carved into monuments
iteration – repetition
seamark – the point of land where a sea journey ends
fell – cruel